BARCELONA

POCKET GUIDE

Walking Eye
mobile app

Discover the world's best destinations with the Insight Guides Walking Eye app, available to download for free in the App Store and Google Play.

The container app provides easy access to fantastic free content on events and activities taking place in your current location or chosen destination, with the possibility of booking, as well as the regularly-updated Insight Guides travel blog: Inspire Me. In addition, you can purchase curated, premium destination guides through the app, which feature local highlights, hotel, bar, restaurant and shopping listings, an A to Z of practical information and more. Or purchase and download Insight Guides eBooks straight to your device.

TOP 10 ATTRACTIONS

LA RAMBLA
A lively and entertaining place by day or night. See page 25.

SAGRADA FAMÍLIA
Gaudí's unfinished masterpiece. See page 55.

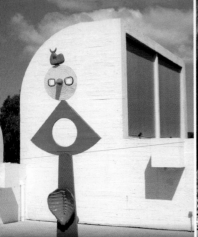

FUNDACIÓ JOAN MIRÓ
This museum showcases an exceptional body of the artist's work. See page 70.

MONESTIR DE PEDRALBES
A peaceful haven. See page 73.

MUSEU PICASSO
The largest collection of the artist's work outside Paris. See page 46.

CASA BATLLÓ
One of the city's famous modernista buildings. See page 51.

PALAU NACIONAL
This monumental building houses 1,000 years of Catalan art. See page 67.

PALAU DE LA MÚSICA CATALANA
Fabulous mosaics, tiles and sculpture. See page 47.

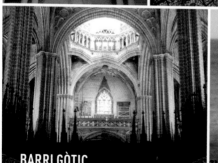

BARRI GÒTIC
The sombre Gothic Cathedral is at the heart of this old quarter. See page 32.

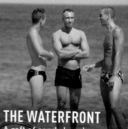

THE WATERFRONT
A raft of sandy beaches makes this a playground for the locals. See page 58.

A PERFECT DAY

9.00am

La Rambla

Get an early start on La Rambla to enjoy it before the crowds arrive. Pick up your newspaper from a newsstand then pop into La Boqueria market – at its most colourful in the morning – for a proper Catalan breakfast like baby squid and poached eggs at El Quim (see page 106).

12 noon

Santa Maria del Mar church

On the other side of Via Laietana is the El Born district. Glimpse the breathtaking interior of Santa Maria del Mar, or sip *una copa de cava* on the terrace of La Vinya del Senyor (see page 107) and admire the church facade.

1.30pm

Lunch time

Get into the local rhythm and have a *menú del dia*, three courses at remarkably good prices, in a neighbourhood bar like Rodrigo (see page 106) in Argenteria, or around the Passeig del Born. Alternatively walk 10 minutes to Barceloneta, for a paella by the sea at Can Majó (see page 110).

10.30am

Gothic Quarter

Across La Rambla is the Gothic Quarter. Meander through its shady, narrow lanes and palm-filled courtyards. Explore the history of the old town at the City History Museum (MUHBA) or break for coffee in the diminutive Meson del Café on Llibreteria.

IN BARCELONA

5.30pm

Explore the Eixample

A session of retail therapy in the modernista setting of the Eixample is recommended for all the family. Those who don't wish to shop can visit a Gaudí building, like La Pedrera or Casa Batlló, or just wander around the area to admire the wealth of decorative details, from stained glass to ceramics, by his contemporaries.

3.30pm

Siesta

A gentle stroll along the Passeig Marítim towards the Vila Olímpica, pausing for coffee in one of the waterfront *xiringuitos* (beach bars), is ideal for working off lunch. Indulge in a taxi back to base for a reviving siesta, essential if you are to keep up the pace until the small hours.

10.30pm

On the town

Round off the day in style, just up the road at designer club Ommsession (Rosselló 265), part of award-winning Hotel Omm, where you can rub shoulders with the beau monde. Alternatively, catch a cab to Mirablau, halfway up Tibidabo hill, which overlooks the city, and dance till dawn.

8.30pm

Drinks and tapas

Relax at one of the many terrace bars in elegant Rambla Catalunya, or try the eponymous cocktail at Dry Martini (Aribau 162), before going for tapas – the perfect dinner, especially when created by top chef Carles Abellan at Tapas 24 (see page 109).

CONTENTS

INTRODUCTION

Barcelona may be the second city of Spain, locked in eternal rivalry with Madrid, but it ruled an empire long before Spain was even born. Some 2,000 years ago, the Romans, on their way to conquering the whole of Iberia, built a forbidding wall around their settlement on the Mediterranean coast and called it Barcino.

Although a visitor could spend days wandering the Gothic Quarter, an atmospheric tangle of medieval buildings and alleyways where the city's glorious past is palpable, Barcelona is anything but a musty old history lesson. It is a dynamic, creative, and daringly modern metropolis.

Once just a grey industrial port, Barcelona has reinvented itself. Rundown neighbourhoods were revived, numerous urban spaces filled with sculpture and greenery was created. The airport, railway, and metro have been brought up to date, and new hotels, museums, and concert halls have sprung up. The most important physical change, though, has been Barcelona's reorientation

⊙ SARDANES

The city – and the region – takes its culture seriously. Rituals like the *sardana*, a traditional dance performed on Saturday evening and Sunday morning in front of the cathedral, and in Plaça Sant Jaume on some Sunday evenings, are held almost sacred. Men, women and children hold hands and form a circle to perform the seemingly simple but highly regimented steps. The band, called a *cobla*, comprising strings, brass and a drum, plays lilting, melancholic tunes as more and more circles form until the entire area is filled with dancers.

towards the sea. With a dynamic port that is now one of the busiest cruise ship stops in Europe, the Port Olímpic, a further leisure port at Diagonal Mar, its clean beaches and renowned seafront neighbourhoods, the Catalan capital has succeeded in marrying the pleasures of the Mediterranean with the sophisticated, creative energy of modern Europe. The focus is now on the two main arteries running east-west to the sea, Avinguda Diagonal and Avinguda Paral.lel. The aim is to create a connection between these two roads and the flourishing port with its cruise-ship terminal, and the Forum's trade fair, exhibition and conference venues.

Tree-lined La Rambla

CATALAN CULTURE

Barcelona's physical transformation has accompanied a rebirth of Catalan culture, long marginalised – often overtly repressed – by Spanish rulers. The most ruthless aggression came during the Franco dictatorship, which lasted from the Spanish Civil War of 1936–39 until the dictator's death in 1975. Under the 1979 Statute of Autonomy, Catalonia regained a substantial measure of self-government. Regardless of the political winds, Catalan arts, literature and language are vigorously promoted by the Catalan government.

Reawakened, too, is the pride the Barceloneses take in their city. The man behind much of it is the city's most famous son,

Antoni Gaudí (1852–1926), one of the creators of *modernisme* – Catalan Art Nouveau. Gaudí's buildings still startle: his soaring, unfinished cathedral, La Sagrada Família, is his best-known work, but there are scores more in Barcelona. Around the turn of the 20th century, a group of *modernistas*, including Lluís Domènech i Montaner and Josep Puig i Cadafalch, dreamed up the most fanciful buildings their rich imaginations and equally rich patrons would allow. More recent architectural stars include Oriol Bohigas, Enric Ruiz-Geli, Miralles and Tagliabue and a host of international architects like Jean Nouvel, Norman Foster, Richard Rogers, Frank Gehry, Herzog and de Meuron, who have all created new landmarks in the city or have work in progress.

DESIGN AND PRAGMATISM

Barcelona also nurtured the careers of some of the 20th-century's greatest artists – the Catalans Joan Miró and Salvador Dalí, and also Pablo Picasso, who spent his formative years in the Catalan capital before seeking fame in Paris (Barcelona's Picasso museum has the largest collection of his work outside Paris). Few other cities are as design-mad as Barcelona. The opening of every high-tech museum, bridge and bar is a public event, design shops do a roaring trade, and avant-garde public spaces more often than not, publicly funded.

However, Barcelona is serious about work and money. Containing 15 percent of Spain's population (1.7 million in the city itself), Catalonia produces more

Take a tour

To quickly get the full measure of this dynamic Mediterranean city, hop on (and off wherever you want) the Bus Turístic, or go for a walking, bike, boat, scooter or helicopter tour. Check www.barcelonaturisme.com for the latest offers.

than 20 percent of the country's GDP and a third of all exports. Catalans have a reputation for being tight with money – a criticism that's a backhanded compliment acknowledging that they know how to earn and manage it.

CATALAN INDEPENDENCE

Barcelona has long been considered different from the rest of Spain. The city is famous for its stubborn sense of independence and identity. Catalans have held onto their language tenaciously, defending it against repeated attempts from Castile, and the Franco government, to extinguish it. Above all, they believe Catalonia is a nation, not just a region. While many would prefer Barcelona to be the capital of an independent, Catalan-speaking nation, having gone so far as declaring independence in 2017, the majority of these hard-working people are simply frustrated that so much locally-generated wealth is re-routed to Madrid.

All political considerations are cast aside, though, when seemingly the whole of Barcelona takes to the streets just before lunch or in the early evening. La Rambla is packed with locals and visitors. Boisterous patrons spill out of corner bars, where they've dipped in to have tapas. Mime artists strike poses for photos and spare change, and older people take a seat to watch the whole parade stream by.

Easygoing beach life

EXPLORING ON FOOT

Barcelona is an ideal city for walking. Hemmed in by the sea, the River Besòs and hills on two sides, the city is surprisingly manageable. It spills down a gentle slope to the waterfront. Near the water are the Barri Gòtic (Gothic Quarter) and the rest of the old city, a labyrinth of streets inhabited for a thousand years. Ancient stones of the Roman city are visible in columns and walls, and you can visit the settlement's original foundations beneath the Museu d'Història de la Ciutat. Barcelona grew out of its original walls, and its modern sectors extend in all directions. The avenues are broad and leafy, punctuated by squares crowded with cafés. The Eixample district, a grid of streets laid out in the 19th century, includes landmark *modernista* apartment buildings, fashionable boutiques, galleries, restaurants and hotels.

Barcelona is every bit as spirited at night as it is during the day. Residents begin their evenings with tapas and rounds of drinks after work, putting dinner off until late (10pm is normal). Live-music venues and clubs don't really get going until 2am. Any day of the week, La Rambla pulsates with life. If late-night Barcelona is too much for you, an evening stroll is rewarding: the cathedral, churches, palaces and monuments are all illuminated. The Barri Gòtic retreats into silence, broken only by the animated hollering of late-night revellers or the rumble of skateboards.

A BRIEF HISTORY

Barcelona was originally called Barcino, named after the Carthaginian general and father of Hannibal, Hamilcar Barca, who established a base on the northeastern coast of Iberia in the 3rd century BC. Phoenicians and Greeks had previously settled the area, and Barcino occupied the site of an earlier Celtiberian settlement called Laie. But the Romans, who conquered all of Iberia, left the most indelible marks on Barcelona. They defeated the Carthaginians at Ilipa in 206 BC and ruled Spain for the next 600 years, a period in which Roman law, language and culture took firm root across the peninsula. The Roman citadel in Barcelona, surrounded by a massive wall, occupied high ground where the cathedral, Catalan government building and city hall now stand. From the 1st century AD Christian communities spread throughout Catalonia.

VISIGOTHIC CAPITAL

After the sack of Rome, Visigoths swept into Spain in AD 476. They made Barcelona their capital from 531 until 554, when they moved their power base to Toledo. The invasion of the Moors in 713 brought the Visigothic kingdom to an end, and Catalonia was briefly overrun by the invaders from North Africa. After their defeat beyond the Pyrenees by the Franks in 801, the Moors withdrew to the south, and retained no lasting foothold in Catalonia.

Catalan character

While much of Spain was under Moorish domination, Catalonia remained linked to Europe. This has done much to determine the distinctive Catalan character.

A feudal lord, Guifré el Pelós (Wilfred the Hairy) became the Count of Barcelona. In 878 he founded a dynasty that would rule for nearly five centuries. He also gave the budding nation its flag of four horizontal red stripes on a gold field, the oldest still in use in Europe. When King Louis V refused to come to their aid against Moorish raiders, the counts of Barcelona declared their independence in 988, a date celebrated as Catalonia's birth as a nation-state. The Catalan nation was soon enlarged through marriage and military adventure, in particular by Ramon Berenguer III, who ruled from 1082 to 1131.

MERCANTILE NATION

Successive generations turned their attention towards the conquest of the Mediterranean basin. Jaume I (1213–76) consolidated control over the Balearic Islands and claimed Valencia. Sicily was annexed in 1282, and over the ensuing century Barcelona reached the peak of its glory. Its mercantilist trade grew rapidly and its territories included Sardinia, Corsica, Naples and Roussillon in southern France.

Columbus' riches

In 1493, after Columbus' voyage to the Americas, he was received by King Ferdinand and Queen Isabella in Barcelona's Palau Reial Major (Royal Palace). Despite the gesture, Castile – the power centre of Spain – exclusively exploited these New World riches, to the exclusion of Barcelona.

The Middle Ages, from the late 13th to the 15th century, was a time of significant building in Barcelona, giving rise to the cathedral and other great Gothic palaces and monuments. Barcelona also served as a channel for the exchange of scientific knowledge and scholarship between the Arab world and the west. The arts flourished, patronised by a vigorous class of artisans, bankers and merchants, including an important Jewish community.

Nascent political institutions appeared, and in 1359 the Corts Catalanes, or Catalan parliament, which had been meeting irregularly since the 1280s, was officially appointed. A body which later became the Generalitat (government) was set up to regulate financial and political concerns.

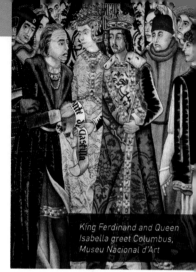
King Ferdinand and Queen Isabella greet Columbus, Museu Nacional d'Art

SPAIN UNITED

The marriage of Ferdinand of Aragón-Catalonia (Ferrán II to the Catalans) to Isabella of Castile in 1469 joined the two crowns and formed the nucleus of a united Spanish state. Under the Catholic Monarchs Catalonia was incorporated into Castile. The Catholic church's hard-line Inquisition expelled Jews from Spain and the thriving communities in Barcelona and Girona were particularly badly affected.

During the 16th century, a Golden Age for Spain, the political influence of Catalonia and Barcelona declined even further. The Habsburg grandson of Ferdinand and Isabella was anointed Carlos I of Spain in 1516. He inherited the title of Holy Roman Emperor and became Charles V, with duties across Europe that gave him little time for Spain.

Showcasing the maritim empire's glory in the Museu Marítim

WAR AND RESISTANCE

In 1640, with Spain and France involved in the Thirty Years' War, Catalonia declared itself an independent republic, allied to France. Spanish troops besieged and captured Barcelona in 1651 and, after the French defeat in 1659, Catalan territories north of the Pyrenees were ceded to France, fixing the border where it is today. The ensuing years were rife with wars and disputes over succession to the crown, in which Barcelona automatically sided with whichever faction opposed Madrid.

The worst of these episodes came in the War of the Spanish Succession (1701–14) between the backers of Philip of Anjou, grandson of Louis XIV of France, and the Habsburg claimant, Archduke Charles of Austria. Charles was enthusiastically received when he landed in Catalonia, but Philip, supported by France, won the war and became the first Bourbon ruler, Philip V. After a 13-month siege, on 11 September 1714 the royal army captured and sacked Barcelona. The Catalan Generalitat was dissolved and the city's privileges abolished. The Ciutadella fortress was built to keep the populace subdued, and official use of the Catalan language was outlawed. Catalonia celebrates this date as its national holiday, the Diada, a symbol of the spirit of nationalist resistance.

Discord within the Spanish government or conflict with foreign powers frequently served as an excuse for Catalan separatists to rise up, though their rebellions were usually summarily squashed. From 1808 to 1814, Spain again became a battleground, with British forces opposing Napoleon in the Peninsular War. Napoleon attacked and destroyed Catalonia's sacred shrine, the monastery at Montserrat.

The spirit of European liberalism was late in reaching Spain. After many reverses, a republic, a constitutional monarchy and a democratic constitution were instituted in 1873. Shortly afterwards, Barcelona was at long last given the right to trade with the colonies of the New World.

INDUSTRIALISATION

Meanwhile, the city had gone about its business, devoting its energies to industrialisation. Barcelona's medieval walls were torn down to make way for expansion in the mid-19th century. The Eixample district was laid out on a grid of broad avenues where the new industrialists built mansions. Wealthy patrons supported architects such as Antoni Gaudí and Lluís Domènech i Montaner. Prosperity was accompanied by a revival in arts and letters, a period known in Catalan as the Renaixença (Renaissance). The city bid for worldwide recognition with the Universal

Montjuïc

Despite the Primo de Rivera dictatorship (1923–30), Barcelona plunged into preparations for the 1929 International Exhibition, with the creation of monumental buildings and sports facilities on the hill of Montjuïc, many of which can still be seen today. It opened just before the Wall Street Crash.

Exposition of 1888, on the site of the Ciutadella fortress, today's Parc de la Ciutadella.

With the industrial expansion, an urban working class evolved. Agitation for social justice and regional ferment created a combustible atmosphere, and the city became the scene of strikes and violence. In 1914 a provincial government, the Mancomunitat, was formed, uniting the four Catalan provinces – Barcelona, Tarragona, Lleida and Girona. It was dissolved in 1923 by General Primo de Rivera, who established a military dictatorship and banned the Catalan language.

CIVIL WAR

In 1931, the Second Republic was established, and King Alfonso XIII escaped to exile. Catalonia won a charter establishing home rule, restoration of the regional parliament and flag, and recognition of Catalan as the official language. Elements in the Spanish army rebelled in 1936, initiating the brutal Civil War. Many churches in Barcelona were put to the torch by anti-clerical mobs. The firmly Republican city was a rallying point for the International Brigade. Barcelona was one of the last cities to fall to the rebel troops of General Francisco Franco at the war's end in 1939.

Aerial view of the city after bombing by the Italian Air Force, 1938

The Civil War ended with some 700,000 combatants dead; another 30,000 were executed, including many priests and nuns; perhaps as many as 15,000 civilians were killed in air raids and numerous refugees left the country. Catalonia paid a heavy price in defeat. Franco abolished all regional institutions and established central controls. The Catalan language was proscribed, even in schools and churches. For years, Barcelona received little financial support from Madrid, and Spain as a whole remained essentially cut off from the rest of Europe.

1960 ONWARDS

Despite this cultural and political repression, by the 1960s the industrious Catalans were again forging ahead, making this corner of Spain the most economically successful in the country. The traditional textile sector was overtaken by the more prosperous iron, steel and chemical industries, which called for manpower, so people from the less prosperous rural regions of Spain flocked to Barcelona. Sprawling suburbs with ugly high-rise buildings mushroomed around the city in an uncontrolled fashion. Franco's government also promoted tourism in the 1960s, and crowds from the North began to descend on the Costa Brava. Speculators exploited the coastline and the economy boomed.

The dictatorship ended with Franco's death in 1975. Juan Carlos, grandson of Alfonso XIII, became king and Spain made a rapid and successful transition to democracy. In Barcelona, cava flowed in the streets on the day Franco died and the Generalitat was restored as the governing body of the autonomous region. The Catalan language was made official and a renaissance of culture and traditions has followed, seen in literature, theatre, television, films, cultural centres, arts festivals and popular fiestas.

In Barcelona the charismatic Socialist mayor, Pasqual Maragall, shaped today's modern city by using the 1992 Olympics as an excuse to start a radical programme of urban reform to remedy years of neglect by central government. The momentum of this drive continued after the Olympics and launched Barcelona into the 21st century, under Mayor Jordi Hereu. Urban, economic and social refurbishment has been implemented in the 22@ project – approved by the city council in 2000 and still ongoing – clearing old industrial areas such as Poble Nou, improving transport links and making way for high-tech industries and classy new business hotels. Despite hard economic times, which have slowed the building process, Barcelona enjoys a high profile status as a top business and conference centre and ranks high amongst European cities for its quality of life.

Recent years have been marked by ongoing development and modernisation of the city as well as rising tensions between the Catalan authorities, led by nationalist Artur Mas and his successor Carles Puigdemont, and the central government in Madrid. Successive Catalan cabinets have been pushing strongly for secession from Spain with the Catalan assembly passing a controversial 18-month 'roadmap' to independence at the beginning of 2016. In 2017 and 2018, this unfolded in full blown crisis as the Catalonian leaders backed an independence referendum which was declared illegal by the government in Madrid. Eventually direct rule was imposed, Puigdemont fled the country, and Spain issued a European Arrest Warrant for his return while many Catalan leaders were arrested and some charged with rebellion. The issue of independence will not dissipate any time soon.

HISTORICAL LANDMARKS

AD 531–54 Barcelona becomes the capital of the Visigoths.

711 Moorish invasion of Spain. They remain there till 1492.

1096–1131 Ramón Berenguer III extends Catalan empire.

1359 Corts Catalanes (Parliament of Catalonia) established.

1469 Ferdinand and Isabella unite Aragón and Castile.

1701–14 War of Spanish Succession.

1713–14 Siege of Barcelona by Felipe V's forces; Ciutadella fortress built.

1888 Barcelona hosts its first Universal Exposition.

1914 Mancomunitat (provincial government) formed in Catalonia.

1923 General Primo de Rivera bans Catalan language.

1932 Catalonia granted short-lived statute of independence.

1936–9 Civil War ends in Franco's rule and isolation of Spain.

1975 Franco dies; Juan Carlos becomes king.

1979 Statute of Autonomy; Catalan restored as official language.

1986 Spain joins European Community (European Union).

1992 Barcelona hosts the Olympics.

2006 A new statute is passed, giving Catalonia more autonomy.

2009 High-tech business district 22@ forges ahead successfully.

2011 Xavier Trias of the Catalan Nationalist party is elected mayor.

2014 80 percent of voters say 'yes' to Catalonia's separation from Spain in a non-binding referendum.

2015 Regional and municipal elections result in a shake-up of the Catalonian political scene. Ada Colau, a social activist, becomes mayor.

2016 Carles Puigdemont embarks on a campaign for independence.

2017 On 17 August 2017, 13 people are killed and 130 are injured when a van is deliberately driven into pedestrians on La Rambla.

2018 Spain withdraws its European Arrest Warrant for Carles Puigdemont after a German court rules that he cannot be extradited for rebellion.

2020 Spanish Grand Prix, one of the world's oldest, is to be held at the Circuit de Barcelona-Catalunya.

2026 Expected completion date of Sagrada Família, 100 years after Gaudi's death.

The Magic Fountain light show, Palau Nacional

 # WHERE TO GO

Barcelona can be approached by neighbourhood or by theme. You can set out to see the Gothic Quarter, Montjuïc hill, or the waterfront, or you can create a tour around the works of Gaudí and *modernisme* or the latest cutting-edge architecture. It's very tempting to try to sandwich everything into your stay, but leave time to get side-tracked in a colourful food market or an alley of antiques shops, or to peek into a quiet courtyard. Take a breather, sit at a pavement café while you linger over a drink, read a book, and watch the world go by.

In the Old Town – Barri Gòtic, La Ribera, El Raval, La Rambla – and the Eixample district, the best way to travel is on foot. For sights further afield, including Montjuïc, Barceloneta and the waterfront, Tibidabo, and two of the top Gaudí attractions, La Sagrada Família and Park Güell, it's best to make use of Barcelona's excellent public transport network – clean and efficient metro, suburban trains, modern buses, funiculars, trams and cable cars – as well as plenty of inexpensive taxis (see page 131). A good map is essential, but it's easy to be fooled by how close things look on paper.

LA RAMBLA

To call **La Rambla ❶** a street is to do it woeful injustice. Perhaps Europe's most famous boulevard – energetic, artistic, demo-cratic and a touch decadent – it is an intoxicating parade of humanity. You will no doubt want to sample it several times during your stay, despite the crowds. It's at its best in the morn-ing or in the early evening, while in the wee hours it's popu-lated by a motley mix of newspaper sellers, street-sweepers and late-night revellers stumbling back to their apartments and hotels. At all times, be streetwise to avoid pickpockets.

The broad, tree-shaded promenade stretches nearly 1.5km (1 mile) down a gentle incline from the city's hub, Plaça de Catalunya (see page 54), to the waterfront. La Rambla takes its name from an Arabic word meaning a sandy, dry river bed; it was a shallow gully until the 14th century, when Barcelona families began to construct homes nearby. As the area became more populated, the stream was soon paved over. To the north of La Rambla (left as you walk down it) is the Gothic Quarter; to the south, or right, is El Raval.

CANALETES

The five sections of La Rambla change in character, as they do in name (hence it is often called 'Les Rambles'), as you stroll along. The short **Rambla de Canaletes** at the top, named after the **Font de Canaletes**, the fountain that is one of the symbols of the city, is where crowds pour in from the Plaça de Catalunya or emerge from the metro and railway stations beneath. On Sunday and Monday in football season you'll find noisy knots of fans verbally replaying the games of Barça, Barcelona's beloved football club; if an important match has just been won, watch out for the fireworks. Here, too, begin the news-stands where you can buy a selection of foreign newspapers and magazines, as well as books – a reflection of Barcelona's status as Spain's publishing centre.

BIRDS AND FLOWERS

Next is **Rambla dels Estudis**, popularly called **Rambla dels Ocells** (Rambla of the Birds) because here the boulevard becomes an outdoor aviary where winged creatures of all descriptions are sold. When the vendors leave at the end of the

The vibrant atmosphere of La Rambla is palpable

day, their cage-lined stalls are folded and shut like wardrobes, with the birds rustling about inside.

Birds give way to flowers in the **Rambla de les Flors**, officially the **Rambla de Sant Josep**. People flock here on 23 April, the feast day of Sant Jordi (St George), patron saint of Catalonia, celebrated as Day of the Book because it is also the anniversary of Cervantes' and Shakespeare's deaths in 1616. A woman traditionally gives her man a book, and a man gives a woman a rose – both of which are available in abundance along La Rambla. Keep an eye peeled on the right side of the road for the delectable *modernista* pastry and chocolate shop, **Escribà** (Antiga Casa Figueres; www.escriba.es), its fanciful swirls on the outside a match for the delicacies within. An ideal spot for coffee.

Facing the Rambla is the elegant **Palau de la Virreina** (La Rambla 99; http://ajuntament.barcelona.cat/lavirreina/ca; Tue–Sun 11am–8pm; free), a grand palace completed in 1778 for the young widow of the viceroy of colonial Peru. The palace is partially open for cultural events and major exhibitions, and houses a branch of the city's Department of Culture where you can find out what cultural events are on in the city, and buy tickets for performances and exhibitions.

LA BOQUERIA

On the right-hand side of the street is one of La Rambla's great attractions: the **Mercat de Sant Josep**, usually called **La Boqueria ②** (www.boqueria.barcelona; Mon–Sat 8am–8pm). This ornate, 19th-century covered market is a cornucopia of delights for the senses: fresh fish, meats, sausages, fruits and vegetables, all kinds of spices, neatly braided ropes of garlic, sun-dried tomatoes and peppers, preserves and sweetmeats, to make a gourmand swoon. La Boqueria is also a vibrant community, where shoppers and merchants greet each other by name, ribald sallies across the aisles set off gales of laughter, and the freshness of the *rape* (an angler fish popular in Catalonia) is debated with passion.

The huge market is laid out under high-ceilinged ironwork naves, like a railway station. Restaurants in and near the market are like first-aid stations for those who become faint with hunger. The best time to visit is when practised shoppers and restaurateurs go – early in the morning.

The heart of the Rambla is nearby, at the Pla de la Boqueria, a busy intersection near the Liceu metro station paved with an unmistakable Joan Miró mosaic. Here stands one of Europe's great opera houses, the **Gran Teatre del Liceu** (www.liceubarcelona.cat; 45 minute tours Mon–Fri every hour from 2pm–5pm, Sat from 11am, 30 minute tours from Mon–Sat at 1pm), inaugurated in 1861. Montserrat Caballé and Josep Carreras made their reputations singing at this theatre, a monument of the Catalan Renaissance and favourite haunt of the Catalan

La Boqueria market

elite. The opera house was gutted by a fire in 1994 then stunningly restored and extended, and eventually reopened in 1999.

Directly across the Rambla is the Cafè de l'Òpera (www.cafe operabcn.com), a handsome, *modernista*-style café that's always busy and retains a local feel although it is also popular with visitors. It's a good spot for refreshment before you push on down the **Rambla dels Caputxins**. The Rambla's character, like the incline, goes downhill after the Liceu, but the street-entertainment factor rises in inverse proportion. Wade your way through jugglers, human statues, fire-eaters, tarot-card readers, lottery-ticket sellers, hair-braiders and street artists rapidly knocking out portraits, caricatures and chalk master-works on the pavement.

PALAU GÜELL

On the right side of the street is the **Hotel Oriente** (see page 135), which preserves a 17th-century Franciscan convent

Mosaic chimney on Gaudí's Palau Güell

and cloister inside. Note the naïve painted angels floating over the doorway of what was Ernest Hemingway's favourite Barcelona lodging. Just beyond, on Carrer Nou de la Rambla is **Palau Güell ❸** (www.palauguell.cat; Apr–Sept Tue–Sat 10am–8pm, till 5.30pm rest of the year), the mansion that Gaudí (see page 54) built in 1885 for his principal patron, textile tycoon Count Eusebi Güell. This extraordinary building is structured around an enormous salon, from which a conical roof covered in mosaic tiles emerges to preside over an unusual landscape of capriciously placed battlements, balustrades and strangely shaped chimneys.

PLAÇA REIAL

Returning to the Rambla, cross over into the arcaded **Plaça Reial**. This handsome, spacious square is graced with a fountain, palm trees, and wrought-iron lamp-posts designed by the young Gaudí. Like the Boqueria market and other landmarks, this square came into being as a result of the destruction of a convent, when church property was expropriated in the mid-19th century. Plaça Reial is a fun and lively place, lined with bars, cafés and restaurants that offer pavement seating, and is buzzing with action night and day.

Leading down to the harbour is the short **Rambla de Santa Mònica**, beginning at the Plaça del Teatre, site of the Teatre Principal. The warren of alleys to the right, once known as the **Barri Xino**, while cleaned up a bit, is still pretty seedy and not the best place for a midnight stroll, but some of the old bars are becoming fashionable again, while the atmospheric Pastís bar has not changed in decades.

Carrer dels Escudellers, a busy pedestrian street on the other side of the Rambla, is the gateway to a district of clubs, bars, restaurants and trendy boutiques, and the delights of the Gothic Quarter. At its far end, Plaça George Orwell has become a trendy place to congregate.

Back on La Rambla, **Centre d'Art Santa Mònica** (http://artssantamonica.gencat.cat; Tue–Sat 11am–9pm, Sun

Palm-lined Plaça Reial

The Catedral façade

11am–5pm; free) is an avant-garde contemporary arts centre in a 17th-century convent.

Nearer the port is the **Museu de Cera** ❹ (www.museocerabcn.com; summer daily 10am–10pm, winter Mon–Fri 10am–1.30pm, 4–7.30pm, Sat–Sun 11am–2pm, 4.30–8.30pm), a tourist trap with 300-plus wax effigies in a neo-classical styled building, that also houses a fantasy 'forest café'. La Rambla ends at the broad, open space facing the **Mirador de Colom**, a statue honouring Christopher Columbus, where an elevator ascends to the top (daily 8.30am–8.30pm) for good views of the port. Just beyond lies Barcelona's revitalised waterfront.

BARRI GÒTIC

From its beginnings more than 2,000 years ago, Barcelona has grown outwards in concentric rings, like ripples on a pond. The ancient core is a hill the Romans called Mont Tàber, where they raised a temple to Augustus Caesar and in the 4th century AD built high walls about 1.5km (1 mile) long to protect their settlement. This is the nucleus of the medieval district called the **Barri Gòtic** or Gothic Quarter, with its remarkable concentration of medieval palaces and churches, many built on Roman foundations.

THE CATEDRAL

The best place to begin a tour is the superb **Catedral** ❺ (www.
catedralbcn.org; Mon-Fri 8am-7.30pm, Sat-Sun 8.30am-8pm,
hours vary between worship and tourist visits; free during worship hours, charge for seeing the choir and the roof), the neighbourhood's focal point. It was begun in 1298 on the site of earlier
churches going back to the times of the Visigoths. The final touch
– the florid Gothic facade – was not completed until the end of
the 19th century and thus contrasts with the simple, octagonal
towers. The ribs of the cathedral's high vault are joined at carved
and painted keystone medallions, a typically Catalan feature. In
the centre of the nave is a splendid Gothic choir with lacy spires.

Steps under the altar lead to the alabaster tomb of Santa
Eulàlia, one of the city's two patron saints, martyred in the 4th
century and celebrated with a *Festa Major* in February. On the
wall of the right aisle are the tombs of Count Ramón Berenguer
I and his wife Almodis, who founded an earlier cathedral on this
spot in 1058. The Catalan Gothic altarpieces of the Transfiguration
painted for the Sant Salvador chapel in the 15th century by Bernat
Martorell are considered his masterpiece.

The leafy cloister, which now also contains a gift shop, is a
lively refuge, with birds fluttering among the orange, magnolia
and palm trees and inhabited by 13 geese, symbolising the age
of Eulàlia when she died. Watch where you walk, as the cloister
is paved with tombstones, badly worn, but many still bearing
the ancient emblems of the bootmakers', tailors' and other
craft guilds whose wealth helped pay for the cathedral. From
the cloister, pass to the **Capella de Santa Llúcia**, a chapel with
13th- and 14th-century tombstones on the floor and a monument to an armoured crusader knight on one wall.

Leaving the chapel by its front entrance, turn left into Carrer
del Bisbe. Look up as you walk through the old town to take

Palau de la Generalitat

in the details – a curious hanging sign, a lantern, an unusual sculpture or plants trailing from balconies. On the right is a row of gargoyles leaning from the roof of the Palau de la Generalitat, where there is also a richly ornamented gateway. The lacy overhead bridge is Gothic in style but is actually a 1929 addition.

PLAÇA SANT JAUME

Just ahead is the **Plaça Sant Jaume** ❻, the heart of the Barri Gòtic, where the Government of Catalonia, the Generalitat, faces the Casa de la Ciutat (city hall, also known as the Ajuntament; open Sun 10am–1.30pm, guided tours English; free). Though the institutions they house are not always in agreement, the two buildings are a harmonious pair: both have classical facades that hide their Gothic origins.

The **Palau de la Generalitat**, on the north side of the square, is the more interesting of the two. It dates from 1359, when it was made the executive branch, reporting to the Corts Catalanes (referred to as the 'first parliament in Europe'). The nucleus of the present building is the main patio – pure Catalan Gothic, with an open staircase leading to a gallery of arches on slender pillars. The star feature here is the flamboyant Gothic facade of the **Capella de Sant Jordi**. The **Saló de Sant Jordi**, a vaulted hall in the 17th-century front block of the building, is lined with modern murals of historical scenes. It is open to the only on a few days each year. It is best to check the dates / times and book in advance by using www.president.cat.

The **Ajuntament** (for visits call 934 027 000), across the plaza, has held Barcelona's city hall since 1372. It was here that the Consell de Cent, a council of 100 notable citizens, met to deal with civic affairs under the watchful eyes of the king. The original entrance can be seen around the left corner of the building, on the Carrer de la Ciutat. Inside, the left stair-case leads to the upper gallery of the old courtyard and to the **Saló de Cent** (Hall of the One Hundred) with a barrel-vaulted ceiling. The red-and-yellow bars of Catalonia's flag decorate the walls. The hall where the city council now meets adjoins, and at the head of the black marble staircase is the **Saló de les Cròniques** (Hall of the Chronicles), noted for the modern murals in sepia tones by Josep Maria Sert.

From behind the Ajuntament, take the short Carrer d'Hèrcules to Plaça Sant Just for a peek at the church of **Sants Just i Pastor** and the pretty lit-tle square on which it sits, evocative of a bygone Barcelona. The church is one of the oldest in the city, though it was repeatedly remodelled. It is said that any will sworn before its altar is recognised as valid by the courts of Barcelona, a practice dating from the 10th century.

September festival

The Plaça Sant Jaume is the meeting place for the giants *(gegants)*, the huge regal figures that process through the streets at the festival of La Mercè, one of Barcelona's patron saints (with Santa Eulàlia), in September. It is also where you will see *castells* – human towers reaching nine people high – an at-traction at various fiestas.

The Museu d'idees i invents de Barcelona is no longer open on Carrer de la Ciutat however, if you'd like to take a break for a bit of shopping the Vives de la Cortada, Minerales, Joyería e Inciensos (https://vivescortadaimport.com) has a beautiful collection of stones to purchase or even just to view.

PLAÇA DEL REI

From Plaça Sant Just take Dagueria, cross over Jaume I and follow the street up to Baixada Llibreteria, home to one of Barcelona's oldest and tiniest coffee shops, El Mesón del Café. One block down on the left is Veguer, which leads to the **Plaça del Rei** and the **Museu d'Història de la Ciutat de Barcelona** ❼ (MUHBA; City History Museum; http://ajuntament.barcelona.cat/museuhistoria/ca; Tue–Sat 10am–7pm, Sun 10am–8pm). The building is a Gothic mansion that was moved stone by stone to this location. In the basement, excavations have uncovered a portion of the Roman city, including shops running along the inside of the Roman wall. Dyeing vats for a clothing industry and evidence of wine-making have been unearthed. Most importantly, however, evidence has been revealed of an early church on the site with a bishop's residence, which provides the link between the Roman and medieval cities. A lift takes visitors down to view the subterranean city.

Above them is the **Palau Reial Major** (Royal Palace), which acted as the residence for the Kings of Aragón, and into which you emerge at the end of the excavations. The main buildings here are the chapel, tower and great hall. The **Capella de Santa Àgata** (Chapel of St Agatha) is notable for the 15th-century altarpiece of the *Adoration of the Magi* by one of Catalonia's finest artists, Jaume Huguet.

The vast, barrel-vaulted great hall or throne room, the **Saló del Tinell**, was built for royal audiences in 1359 under Pere III (the Ceremonius) by Guillem Carbonell. On occasion the Corts

Catalanes (Parliament) met here. This is where Ferdinand and Isabella supposedly received Columbus in 1493 on his return from his first voyage to the Americas. It was later used as a church, and by the Inquisition, whose victims were burned at the stake in the square. Concerts are held in the square in summer, notably during the La Mercè fiesta.

Behind the Royal Palace, off Carrer Tapineria, is Plaça de Berenguer el Gran, which has a well-preserved section of the original Roman wall. The defences were 9 metres (30ft) high, 3.5 metres (12ft) thick and marked at intervals by towers 18 metres (59ft) tall. Until 1943, most of this section was covered by old houses, which were removed to restore the walls to view.

TOWARDS THE MUSEU FREDERIC MARÈS

A former wing of the palace that encloses the Plaça del Rei was rebuilt in 1557 to become the **Palau del Lloctinent**

A shady courtyard at the Museu Frederic Marès

(Palace of the Lieutenant), residence of the king's representative. It has been beautifully renovated and can now be visited, via an entrance on Carrer dels Comtes. Notice its elegant patio with a noble staircase and remarkable carved wooden ceiling.

Just beyond, flanking the cathedral, is the **Museu Frederic Marès** ❽ (www.museumares.bcn.cat; Tue–Sat 10am–7pm, Sun 11am–8pm; free Sun after 3pm and the first Sun in the month 11am–8pm), which has a beautiful courtyard with an attractive café in the summer months. Marès, a 20th-century sculptor of civic statues, was a compulsive collector who bequeathed to Barcelona an unusually idiosyncratic collection of art consisting of work from the ancient world up through the 19th century. The lower floors of the museum house the sculpture collection. The Collector's Cabinet takes up the second and third floors, described as 'a museum within a museum'.

ROMAN REMAINS AND THE JEWISH GHETTO

Retracing your steps on the narrow street flanking the cathedral, circle around to the rear and duck into the narrow Carrer del Paradís. Here, just inside the doorway of the Centre Excursionista de Catalunya, four columns of the Roman Temple of Augustus are embedded in the wall. This narrow lane takes you back into Plaça Sant Jaume. Streets radiate in all directions, each an invitation to explore the Barri Gòtic. The **Carrer del Call** leads into the labyrinth of narrow streets that was the Call, or Jewish Quarter, until the late 14th century. Today the quarter bustles with antiques shops and dealers of rare books, plus bars and restaurants frequented by antiquarians and artists. Just off St Domènec del Call is the **Centre d'Interpretació del Call** (Placeta de Mannel Ribé; Tue–Fri 11am–2pm, Sat–Sun 11am–7pm; free), a branch of the history museum and an information centre on this historic area.

⊘ EL CALL

Barcelona's Jews, though noted as doctors, scholars and jewellers, were confined to El Call and forced to wear long, hooded cloaks with yellow headbands. Taxation of the community was a source of royal income. This did not save El Call from being burned and looted as persecution of the Jews throughout Spain mounted in the 13th and 14th centuries. Eventually the Jews of Barcelona were killed, expelled, or forcibly converted to Christianity, and their synagogues were turned into churches. Just off Carrer del Call, at Carrer de Marlet 1, a medieval inscription in Hebrew marks the site of a hospital founded by one 'Rabbi Samuel Hassareri, may his life never cease'.

Meander into Baixada de Santa Eulàlia. Just off it is the tiny **Plaça Sant Felip Neri**, a peaceful square, where the church was pockmarked by Italian bombs during the Civil War. Boutique hotel Neri, set in two historical houses with one being a 12th-century medieval palace, has a privileged view of the scene.

ANTIQUE ALLEY

The Baixada de Santa Eulàlia descends to **Carrer de Banys Nous**, named for the long-gone 12th-century 'new' baths of the ghetto. This winding street, which more or less follows the line of the old Roman wall, is the unofficial boundary of the Barri Gòtic. It is also known as the Carrer dels Antiquaris – the street of antique dealers. Keep your eyes peeled for unusual hand-painted shop signs, the fretwork of Gothic balconies, and dusty treasures in the shop windows. You will also notice the old tile signs with a cart symbol high on the walls, the indication of one-way streets.

A TRIO OF PLAZAS

Around the corner is a trio of impossibly pretty plazas. **Plaça Sant Josep Oriol** adjoins **Plaça del Pi**, on which sits **Santa Maria del Pi ❾**, a handsome Catalan Gothic church with a tall, octagonal bell tower and a harmonious facade pierced by a large 15th-century rose window. 'Pi' means pine tree, and there is a small one here replacing the landmark specimen of past centuries. Buildings in the plaza show the *sgrafitto* technique of scraping designs in coloured plaster, imported from Italy in the early 1700s. Barcelona's emerging merchant class favoured such facades as an inexpensive substitute for the sculptures on aristocratic palaces.

These adjoining squares, together with the smaller **Placeta del Pi** to the rear of the church, are the essence of old Barcelona and a great place to while away the hours. The bars with tables spread out under leafy trees in each of the

Inside Santa Maria del Pi

squares are magnets for young people and visitors, who are entertained by roving musicians. On Saturdays and Sundays, artists typically offer their canvases for sale in lively Plaça Sant Josep Oriol, where the Bar del Pi is a popular meeting place. At weekends, a farmers' market selling cheeses, bread and honey is set up in the Plaça del Pi.

The street that leads north from Plaça del Pi, **Carrer Petritxol**, is one of the Barri Gòtic's most traditional. The narrow alley is lined with art galleries, framing shops and traditional *granjas* – good stops for pastries and hot chocolate. Barcelona's oldest (open since 1877) and most famous art gallery is **Sala Parés** (http://salapares.com) at No. 5.

AROUND PLAÇA NOVA

At Carrer Portaferrisa, a left turn will take you to La Rambla, while a right turn will take you back to the cathedral and a handful of additional sights on the perimeter of the Barri Gòtic. (You could also return to Plaça Sant Josep Oriol and take Carrer de la Palla.) In **Plaça Nova**, in front of the cathedral, is the Col.legi d'Arquitectes (Architects' Association). Picasso designed the graffiti-like drawings of the Three Kings and children bearing palm branches that are etched on the 1960s facade. For three weeks in December, a market selling Nativity figures and Christmas trees occupies the Plaça Nova – a square that got its name, 'New', in 1356 and has held markets for nearly 1,000 years. Look for the strange, quintessential Catalan figure, *el caganer* – the red-capped peasant squatting and defecating beside the manger.

The pedestrian thoroughfare that leads north to Plaça de Catalunya is **Avinguda Portal de l'Àngel**, one of the city's main shopping streets, where you will find major international brands such as Zara and Pull & Bear. It is especially busy when *rebaixes* (sales) are on. Look for little Carrer Montsió, which leads to **Els Quatre Gats** (The Four Cats; see page 106), a bar and restaurant that became famous when Picasso and a group of young intellectuals – painters Ramón Casas and Santiago Rusiñol among them – frequented it. Picasso had his first exhibition here in 1901, and the bar, one of the first commissions for the *modernista* architect Puig i Cadafalch, preserves its turn-of-the-20th-century ambience and is, understandably, a great favourite with visitors to Barcelona.

LA RIBERA

Some of the most beautiful Gothic architecture and most fascinating medieval corners of Barcelona lie just outside the Barri Gòtic on the other side of Via Laietana – a traffic-filled avenue roughly parallel to the Ramblas, which was cut through the city in 1859 to link the port with the modern centre (the Eixample).

The pure Catalan gothic architecture of Santa Maria del Mar

This atmospheric quarter, **La Ribera**, is home to the Museu Picasso and the majestic church of **Santa Maria del Mar** ❿ (for opening hours and guided visits go to www.santamariadelmar barcelona.org). Carrer de l'Argenteria cuts a diagonal swathe from Plaça de l'Angel to the church. Begun in 1329 at the height of Catalonia's expansion as a Mediterranean power, it is the greatest example of pure Catalan Gothic, with unadorned exterior walls, a sober facade flanked by three-tiered octagonal bell towers, and a beautiful rose window over the portal.

The dimensions and austerity of the interior are breathtaking. Fires during Civil War rioting in 1936 consumed all the trappings of chapels, choir and altar, leaving the interior stripped to its essence. The result is a lofty hall suffused with soft light from the stained-glass windows. Three naves are supported by slim, octagonal columns set 13 metres (43ft) apart, and the dimensions of the interior are multiples of this distance, achieving a perfect symmetry. Behind the simple altar, the columns branch high overhead into the arched vaulting of the apse. Keep an eye out for the colourful restored keystones starting at the entrance.

The acoustics are excellent, best demonstrated by the concerts held in the church.

EL BORN

The rear door of the church leads to the **Passeig del Born**, a pretty, rectangular plaza where jousts were held in the Middle Ages and which today is the nucleus of this fashionable area, full of smart galleries, restaurants, bars and chic shops. Many of the little streets surrounding the church are named after the guilds of the craftsmen who once worked here, such as *sombrerers* (hatmakers), *mirallers* (mirror-makers) and *espasería* (sword-makers). The area is better known now for the people who fill

☉ PABLO PICASSO

The world's most acclaimed 20th-century artist, Pablo Ruiz y Picasso was born in 1881 in Málaga, the son of an art teacher, whose work took the family to Barcelona. Picasso began his art studies here and became part of a group of innovative artists and writers. In 1900, Picasso first visited Paris, and settled there four years later. He never returned to Barcelona after 1934. Even had he wanted to do so, his opposition to the Franco regime would have made it impossible, but his work always retained strong Spanish links. When Picasso died in 1973 (two years before the death of Franco and the end of the dictatorship), the bulk of his own collection, now in the Musée Picasso in Paris, went to the French government in a deal to settle taxes.

its designer bars late into the night and spill out onto the streets. At the end, the magnificent, wrought-iron **El Born Centre Cultural or Born CMM** (http://elborncul turaimemoria.barcelona. cat), the old fruit-and-vegetable market, has been converted into a museum and cultural centre. It features the archaeological ruins of a medieval city and aims to show how life was in the city from 1713-1714. The centre also hosts concerts and exhibitions.

Museu Picasso

CARRER MONTCADA AND THE MUSEU PICASSO

One of Barcelona's grandest medieval streets, **Carrer Montcada**, populated by aristocrats from the 14th to the 16th centuries, is lined with splendid Gothic palaces, each with an imposing door or arched gate to an inner courtyard from where an ornamental staircase usually led up to reception rooms. These mansions were gradually abandoned after the demolition of the adjoining district and construction of the Ciutadella fortress. This quarter is the most authentically medieval part of the city. At No. 12, the Museu de Cultures del Món (Museum of Cultures of the World, http://museuculturesmon.bcn.cat; Tue–Sat 10am–7pm, Sun till 8pm) opened in 2015, presents arts and artefacts from all over the non-Western world. The curators' passion for collecting and sharing the artistic wealth is much in evidence here.

Across the street, the **Museu Picasso** ⑪ (www.museupicasso. bcn.es; Tue–Sun 9am–7pm, Thu until 9.30pm; free the first Sun of month and Thursday afternoons from 6pm–9.30pm), occupies five palaces (two used for temporary exhibitions). The main entrance is through the 15th-century **Palau Aguilar**. The buildings were acquired by the city to house the collection of paintings, drawings and ceramics donated by Picasso's lifelong friend and secretary, Jaume Sabartés. After the museum opened in 1963, Picasso added sketches and paintings from his childhood and youth. The earliest works date from his ninth year. As a teenager he produced large canvases in the 19th-century realist style, such as the *First Communion and Science and Charity*.

The collection of his work is the largest outside Paris, and while it doesn't possess any of his finest pieces, it does have two good examples of his Blue Period (1901–4), as well as *The Harlequin* (1917), and the idiosyncratic *Las Meninas* series, the variations on the theme of the Velázquez masterpiece in Madrid's Prado Museum, which provides a fascinating view of Picasso's innovative approach to his subject.

Opposite, down Barra de Fero, the **Museu Europa d'Art Modern** (MEAM; www.meam.es; Tue–Sun 11am–7pm) is a living museum which promotes figurative art from the late 19th century to the present day.

MORE MANSIONS AND MUSEUMS

The **Museu del Disseny** (Disseny Hub Barcelona; Tue–Sun 10am–8pm; http://ajuntament.barcelona.cat), is a centre that merges design museums, research, and production. This hub contains three DHUB museums housed under one roof in the much-vaunted Design Museum in Plaça de les Glòries. Regular exhibitions take place and permanent collections include fashion, textiles, product design and decorative arts.

Stunning Palau de la Música Catalana

All the mansions along Carrer de Montcada here merit a peek in at their courtyards, but one that's always open is the handsome, baroque **Palau Dalmases** (No. 20). On the ground floor is Espai Barroc (Baroque Space), an over-the-top, rococo bar. At the end of the street, in Plaçeta Montcada, you can get wonderful Basque tapas in the Euskal Etxea bar (see page 107).

PALAU DE LA MÚSICA

Up Via Laietana several blocks from Carrer Princesa, at Carrer del Palau de la Música 4–6, is one of the city's greatest achievements of *modernista* architecture, the **Palau de la Música Catalana** ⓬ (www.palaumusica.org; guided tours daily 10am–3pm, July–Aug from 9am, booking advised). Designed by Lluís Domènech i Montaner, and inaugurated in 1908, it is the perfect expression of *modernisme* and has been designated a Unesco World Heritage Site. It is an explosion of mosaics,

tiles, stained glass, enamel, sculpture and carving. The brick exterior, with Moorish arches and columns inlaid with floral tiles, is sober compared to what's inside, where every square inch is embellished.

One of Domènech's main concerns was to let in as much natural light as possible, making the hall light and roomy. The structural skeleton is iron – an innovation in those days – which allows the walls to be made of glass. Sunlight streaming in during afternoon concerts sets the place on fire. On either side of the stage the rich colours of the room are offset by sculpted groups of musical masters in white plaster. Between them, the silvery pipes of a grand organ stand in orderly contrast. A curved wall is covered with mosaics of muses playing instruments; their upper bodies are made of porcelain and seem to emerge magically from the walls. Overhead is the Palau's crowning glory, a magical, stained-glass orb.

The best way to experience the Palau is to attend a concert. Programmes range from classical recitals to jazz (box office tel: 932 957 207; Mon–Sat 9.30am–9pm, 10am–3pm on Sun). The alleyways opposite lead to Santa Caterina market, a dazzling renovation by architects EMTB, creators of the Scottish Parliament building, and a great place to eat.

EL EIXAMPLE

The **Eixample** district, north of Plaça de Catalunya, is the city's main shopping and commercial area. You will probably want to spend a lot of time here if you are interested in Gaudí. The neighbourhood has spectacular apartment blocks, examples of early 20th-century *modernista* architecture, and the central part is known as the **Quadrat d'Or** (Golden Square).

The principal avenues are the elegant Passeig de Gràcia and the Rambla de Catalunya, not to be confused with La Rambla. In a manageable area between the Gran Vía de les Corts Catalanes and Avinguda Diagonal, you'll find most of the *modernista* masterpieces. Barcelona's most visited sight is Gaudí's unfinished cathedra,l La Sagrada Família. On the northern outskirts of the Eixample, it can be easily reached on foot or by metro.

Despite the exuberance of the architecture, the city's 'modern' district is a model of rationalist urban planning, a rigid geometric grid simply called 'the Extension' *(Eixample)*. The outrageous and conservative coexist here without much fuss. Barcelona's expansion came about in a remarkable burst of urban development. By the mid-1800s the city was bursting at the seams and suffocating inside its ring of medieval walls. A competition was held in 1859 to select a plan for a new quarter between the old city and the Collserola hills. The job went to an engineer named Ildefons Cerdà, whose plan quintupled the city's size in a matter

Curvy Casa Batlló

of decades. The Eixample construction transformed Barcelona into a showcase of extravagant *modernista* architecture, and the swanky Passeig de Gràcia became the place to be seen. Barcelona used the 1888 Universal Exposition as an open house to show the world its new face.

THE ILLA DE LA DISCORDIA

The best place to begin a *modernista* tour is on Passeig de Gràcia, with its single, hallucinatory block popularly known as the **Illa de la Discòrdia** ⓭ (Block of Discord), set between Consell de Cent and Aragó. It gained its name because of the three stunning buildings in markedly different architectural styles that are located almost next door to one other.

At No. 35 Domènech i Montaner's impressive **Casa Lleó Morera** (1902–6) incorporates both Moorish and Gothic elements. This grand apartment house (Tue–Sun 10am–7pm; guided tours only tel: 93 676 27 33; www.casalleomorera.com) has suffered some disfigurement, especially on the ground floor, where the Spanish luxury brand Loewe installed picture windows and destroyed several original sculptures. Renovations happen quite regularly, so check before you go to ensure it is open. At No. 41 is the **Casa Amatller** (1900), which was built for a chocolate manufacturer. Puig i Cadafalch drew inspiration from Flanders for the stepped roof covered in glazed tiles. It is now open to visitors (daily 10am–6pm; tel: 93 461 74 60; guided tours only; www.amatller.org). The caretaker's office contains one of the finest stained-glass windows of the *modernista* era.

CASA BATLLÓ

Gaudí's highly personal **Casa Batlló** (1904–6) is next door and can be visited, to the delight of many (www.casabatllo.es; daily 9am–9pm, book online as there is often a queue). The curvy contours, unexpected combinations of textures and materials, bright colours and infinite detail are Gaudí hallmarks, as are the prevalent religious and nationalist symbols. Casa Batlló is said to pay tribute to the patron saint of Catalonia, Sant Jordi, and the dragon he slayed. Gaudí himself left no clues as to his intent. The undulating blue-tile roof certainly looks like a dragon's scaly hide, while the balconies could be the skulls and bones of its victims (others have

⊙ MODERNISME

Modernisme, a movement related to the design styles in vogue in Europe in the late 19th century – French Art Nouveau, German and Austrian Jugendstil – was a rebellion against the rigid forms and colourless stone and plaster of classical architecture. In Barcelona the new style assumed nationalist motifs and significance, which may be why it has been so carefully preserved here. Although there was an entire school of *modernista* architects working in Barcelona from the late 19th century until the 1930s, it is customary to speak of the 'Big Three': Antoni Gaudí, who left such a personal mark on the city; Lluís Domènech i Montaner (Palau de la Música Catalana and Casa Morera); and Josep Puig i Cadafalch (Casa Amatller, Casa Terrades and Els Quatre Gats), all of which are described in this guide.

suggested they are Venetian carnival masks). Sant Jordi's cross and a shaft suggest a spear being thrust into the dragon's back. Casa Batlló's facade is covered with scraps of broken plate and tile, a decorative technique called *trencadís* that Gaudí employed repeatedly. In this case he dramatically remodelled both the exterior and interior of an existing house.

LA PEDRERA

Further up and across the street, at No. 92, is **Casa Milà** ⑭ (tel: 932 142 576; www.lapedrera.com; Mar–early Nov 9am–8.30pm and 9pm–11pm, early Nov–Feb daily 9am–6.30pm and 7pm–9pm), Gaudí's acclaimed apartment block. Known as **La Pedrera** (the stone quarry, an allusion to its rippling, limestone surface), it was built between 1906 and 1910, and has been declared a Unesco World Heritage Site. The sinuous facade, with wonderfully twisted wrought-iron balconies, bends around the corner of Carrer Provença.

The attic floor is now a handsome, high-tech museum (Espai Gaudí) with an interesting exhibition of his work. One of the original apartments (El Pis), all odd shapes, handcrafted door knobs, and idiosyncratic details, has been outfitted with period furniture (many of the pieces designed by Gaudí himself), and can be visited.

La Pedrera had one of the world's first underground parking garages; today the space houses an amphitheatre where cultural conferences are held. The building's owner, the cultural Fundació Caixa de Catalunya, has transformed the first floor into an exhibition space for impressively curated shows.

For many, the wavy rooftop is the highlight, with its decoration of recycled tiles, cluster of swirling Darth Vader-like chimneys, known as 'witch scarers' and spectacular views of Barcelona.

PASSEIG DE GRÀCIA

You are likely to be busy looking up at decorative details or gazing in chic store windows along **Passeig de Gràcia**, but be sure to notice the ground as well: Gaudí designed the hexagonal pavement tiles with nature motifs. The mosaic benches and iron street lamps with little bat motifs (1900) are by Pere Falqués.

Sinuous facade of Casa Milà

There are other numerous examples of *modernisme* throughout the Eixample. Have a look at the streets which cut across Passeig de Gràcia, especially Diputació, Consell de Cent, Mallorca and València. In the old town you'll stumble across marvellous *modernista* store fronts, such as the stamp shop at Carrer dels Boters, the Antiga Casa Figueras pastry shop on the Ramblas and the wonderful dining room of the Hotel España in Carrer Sant Pau. In addition, details of a special route, the Ruta del Modernisme, which visits at least 115 examples, can be found online at www.rutadelmodernisme.com. A guidebook is also available that gives discounts on entrance tickets while all the opening times, prices, and locations can be found on the website.

In addition to the jewels of *modernista* architecture, Passeig de Gràcia and neighbouring Rambla Catalunya are lined with cafés, galleries, bookstores, elegant fashion boutiques and smart hotels. This is definitely the place for designer shopping, for both international and top Spanish names like Adolfo

Dominguez and Catalans Antonio Miró and Armand Basi, as well as high-street fashion, such as that at Zara.

AROUND THE AVENUES

The **Plaça de Catalunya**, where Passeig de Gràcia begins, was designed to be the city's hub, and it is certainly a lively crossroads and meeting place, especially the legendary Café Zurich. The bus, metro, and the regional and national rail systems radiate from this square (see Transport, page 130) and El Corte Inglés department store occupies the whole of the northern side.

Parallel to Passeig de Gràcia is the Rambla de Catalunya, an extension of the Old Town Rambles, lined with smart shops, terrace cafés, restaurants and galleries. Traffic moves down either side of the pedestrianised centre, which is considerably more sedate than the lower Rambles.

⊙ ANTONI GAUDÍ

Count Eusebi Güell, a textile manufacturer, was Gaudí's patient and daring patron, a man who was able to accept the architect's wildly imaginative ideas. The Palau Güell, which Gaudí began in 1885 (see page 30), previews many aspects of his work. Gaudí died in 1926 at the age of 74, and is buried in the crypt of his great cathedral.

He was a deeply pious and conservative man, despite his innovations, and during his last years he lived in a room on the site, obsessed with the project. When passers-by discovered the architect run over by a tram in a nearby street in 1926 and took him to hospital, the doctors, unable at first to identify him, thought the dishevelled old man was a tramp. When it was discovered who he was, the entire city turned out for his funeral.

On Carrer d'Aragó (between Passeig de Gràcia and Rambla Catalunya) is the **Fundació Antoni Tàpies**  (www.fundaciotapies.org; Tue–Sat 10am–7pm, Sun until 3pm), dedicated to the work of Catalonia – and perhaps Spain's – foremost contemporary artist (1923–2012). In addition to Tàpies' own work, it holds excellent temporary exhibitions, a study centre and library, and it is all housed in a

The Sagrada Família's soaring central nave

gorgeous 1880 Domènech i Montaner building – one of the first examples of *modernisme*. From the outside, viewed from across the street, you can appreciate Tàpies' whimsical, tangled wire sculpture *Núvol i Cadira* (Cloud and Chair) on the roof.

LA SAGRADA FAMÍLIA

What the Eiffel Tower is to Paris or the Statue of Liberty is to New York, the soaring spires of the **Sagrada Família** ⑯ (www.sagradafamilia.org; daily Nov–Feb 9am–6m, Mar till 7pm, Apr–Sept 9am–8pm, till 7pm Oct; guided tours available daily) are to Barcelona. Its unmistakable profile, protruding from the city's skyline, is visible from afar. Yet the eight peculiar, cigar-shaped towers are merely the shell of a church that is nearing completion (now expected in 2026). This was Antoni Gaudí's life work, though he didn't really expect to finish it in his lifetime. Gaudí took over traditional, neo-Gothic plans of an earlier architect in 1883 and supervised work on the eastern, Nacimiento (Nativity) facade, one tower, and part of the apse and nave. This facade seems to be the one most faithful to Gaudí's intentions.

Everything has significance and no space is left unfilled. The three doorways, with stonework dripping like stalactites, represent Faith, Hope and Charity, and are loaded with sculptures depicting angel choirs, musicians and Biblical episodes such as the birth of Jesus, the Flight into Egypt, the Slaughter of the Innocents, the Tree of Calvary, and much more. Twelve bell towers, four at each portal, will represent the Apostles; four higher towers, the Evangelists; a dome over the apse the Virgin; and the central spire, which will be 170 metres (560ft) high, the Saviour.

For many years, the church remained much as it was when Gaudí died, but work has been going on since the 1950s – not an easy task, since Gaudí left few plans behind. Ascend one of the towers (by lift or spiral staircase) for an overview. The western Pasión facade (on Carrer de Sardenya), begun in 1952, includes controversial sculptures by Josep Maria Subirachs. Japanese sculptor Etsuro Sotoo's work can be seen on the Nacimiento facade.

Many people believe the temple should have been left as it was, unfinished, as a tribute to the great Gaudí, but the work continues, supervised by Jordi Bonet Armengol, the son of one of Gaudí's aides. In 2010 the central nave was finally covered, resplendent with its tree-like columns and dazzling roof, and the church was consecrated by Pope Benedict XVI.

A short walk along Avinguda de Gaudí is the **Hospital de la Santa Creu i Sant Pau** (tel: 93 291 90 00; Nov–Mar Mon–Sat 9.30am–4.30pm, Sun until 2.30pm, Apr–Oct Mon–Sat 9.30am–6.30pm, Sun until 2.30pm) designed by Domènech i Montaner.

A working hospital until 2009, it is one of *modernisme's* most underrated and least-known works and well worth visiting. A World Heritage Site, it will now house part of the UN University and become an international centre for the Mediterranean.

GRÀCIA AND PARK GÜELL

Gràcia is a district above the Eixample, retaining a village atmosphere with small local shops and its own town square, Plaça de la Vila de Gràcia (formerly Plaça Rius i Taulet). Streets named Llibertat and Fraternitat and a Plaça Revolució reflect a political past. Gràcia is a popular nightspot, known for its *Festa Major*, which runs for seven days starting from around 15 August. On the hills behind Gràcia, **Park Güell ⑰** (Autumn-Winter daily 8.30am–5.30pm, Spring–Summer daily 8am–9.30pm), another wildly ambitious Gaudí project, was planned as a residential community, to be intertwined with nature. Gaudí's patron Eusebi Güell bought 6 hectares (15 acres) here, overlooking the city and the sea, intending to create a kind of English garden suburb. He gave Gaudí carte blanche to produce something original, and for the next 14 years, on and off, the architect let his imagination run wild; much of the design was, however, eventually completed by Josep Maria Jujol. The park undergoes intermittent renovation work which can affect visits.

Two gingerbread pavilions guard the entrance on Carrer d'Olot: the one on the left is a shop, the one on the right an exhibition centre. In front of them is a tiled lizard fountain; supporting columns mimic tree trunks. Ceilings are decorated with fragments of plates, and undulating benches are splashed with colourful ceramic pieces, known as *trencadís*. Beneath the plaza with the benches is the **Saló de les Cent Columnes** (Hall of the One Hundred Columns). There are actually 86, Doric in style, in what was to be the colony's covered market. Dolls' heads, bottles, glasses and plates are stuck in the ceiling mosaics. Only five buildings were completed, one of which Gaudí lived in for many years, now the **Casa-Museu Gaudí** (www.casamuseugaudi.org; daily Apr–Sept 9am–8pm, Oct–Mar 10am–6pm), a museum of his furniture and memorabilia.

The Swallows

A perennial waterfront attraction are the ferries called Golondrinas (Swallows; www.lasgolondrinas.com), moored opposite the Columbus Monument. These boats have been taking passengers round the harbour ever since the 1888 World Exposition.

THE WATERFRONT

Barcelona turned its back on the sea during the 19th century and focused on developing industry. The sea wall where families loved to walk and catch the breeze on stifling summer nights was dismantled. Access to the

The marina at Port Vell

sea was obstructed by warehouses and railway tracks and expansion proceeded towards the hills. Barceloneta, a neighbourhood created in the early 18thcentury between the port and the beach as part of a military initiative, remained a close-knit working-class community. However, things changed with the creation of an ambitious recreational and commercial area along the waterfront in the early 1990s.

MARITIME HERITAGE

Begin a tour of the waterfront at the Columbus Monument, at the foot of the Ramblas. To the right is **Les Reials Drassanes**, begun in 1255, and now housing the beautifully renovated **Museu Marítim** ⓲ (www.mmb.cat; Tue–Sun 10am–8pm, free on Sundays after 3pm). The 16 bays of these great shipyards, which handled more than 30 galleys, launched ships that extended Catalonia's dominion over the Mediterranean from

Tunis to Greece, Sicily, Sardinia and much of the French coast. The museum contains models from the earliest galleys to the cargo and passenger vessels that have made Barcelona their home port. The prize exhibit is a full-size copy of Don Juan of Austria's victorious flagship *La Galera Reial*.

PORT VELL

At the other side of the busy Passeig de Colom is an undulating wooden walkway and footbridge called the **Rambla del Mar,** which stretches across the mouth of the **Port Vell**. It crosses over to the Moll d'Espanya and **Maremàgnum**, a commercial centre with plenty of shops, bars and restaurants – some with terraces which are a great place to sit and watch the harbour activity. Families head for **L'Aquàrium** ⑲ (www.aquariumbcn. com; Mon–Fri 10am–7.30pm, Sat–Sun 8pm, June–Sept until 9pm) one of Europe's largest aquariums, with a spectacular glass tunnel running through its huge Oceanarium. The Oceanarium allows visitors to walk beneath the water for more than 80 metres with just a few inches of glass separating them from the sharks and other sea life above.

The port is busy with yachts, cruise ships and ferries to Mallorca and Italy. Overhead, cable cars link Montjuïc with the Torre de Jaume I and the Torre de Sant Sebastià in Barceloneta. The **World Trade Center**, a hotel and complex of offices designed by I.M. Pei, appears to be floating in the harbour.

On the mainland, the **Moll de la Fusta**, the old wood-loading quay, was transformed into a broad promenade in the 1980s, and redesigned and landscaped after the 1992 Olympics. Where the Moll d'Espanya joins the promenade stands American pop artists Roy Lichtenstein's colourful surrealist sculpture, called the **Barcelona Head** (El Cap de Barcelona).

Heading towards Barceloneta you skirt the **Marina Port Vell**, a harbour for luxury yachts and chic motor cruisers. On the **Moll de Barceloneta**, in a stylishly renovated warehouse complex, the Palau de Mar houses the **Museu d'Història de Catalunya** ⑳ (www.mhcat.cat; Tue–Sat 10am–7pm, Wed until 8pm, Sun 10am–2.30pm), which is fun as well as informative. A restaurant with a stunning view is on the top floor. Along the Passeig Joan de Borbó, which runs parallel to the quay, numerous popular restaurants have outside tables.

BARCELONETA

If you want to eat really good fish, head to Barceloneta, an area for many years separated from the city in spirit as well as by physical barriers of water and rail yards. It was built in the early 18th century to house dis-possessed families when La Ribera district was demolished to make way for the Ciutadella fortress. A robust *barrio* inhabited by fishermen's families, its beaches were scruffy and dominated by flimsy wooden restaurant shacks (*chiringuitos*).

When the area was virtually rebuilt in prepara-tion for the 1992 Olympics, they were wiped out, and many Barceloneses nos-talgically mourn their loss. You can cut through

The Platja Barceloneta in full swing

the grid of narrow streets or walk along the beach to the **Passeig Marítim** and the landscaped promenade running alongside the wooden walkways and scrupulously clean sands of **Platja Barceloneta**. Several modern *chiringuitos* and some good restaurants have now opened on the beach, a popular hangout on summer nights.

OLYMPIC VILLAGE AND BEYOND

Keep walking and you will come to the 1992 Olympic Village, the **Vila Olímpica**, an award-winning development that has blossomed into a smart and vibrant neighbourhood. It is recognisable from afar by two high-rise buildings – one the prestigious Hotel Arts – and Frank Gehry's enormous, shimmering copper fish. As you approach, passing a small park, the gleaming Hospital de Mar and a *modernista* water tower, the promenade here and in the **Port Olímpic** just beyond becomes increasingly lined with bars and restaurants.

Beyond the Olympic Port, a line of metal poles follow a path inland to the Poble Nou district, known for its textile production. Today the factories have been replaced by design studios, office blocks and apartments, and gentrification continues, spreading north and west to meet Avinguda Diagonal.

At the end of the seafront promenade, **Diagonal Mar** and the Parc del Fòrum have formed a hi-tech residential and commercial neighbourhood. The Universal Forum of Cultures was held here on an esplanade jutting out to sea, and is now a venue for music festivals and conventions. In 2011, the landmark triangular Forum Building became home to the **Museu Blau** ❷❶ (Blue Museum; http://museuciencies.cat; Tue–Fri 10am–6pm, Sat until 7pm, Sun 10am–8pm), an interactive natural history and science museum which offers temporary exhibits at the museum and the Botanical Garden.

Museu Blau

PARC DE LA CIUTADELLA

Lodged between the Olympic Village and La Ribera is **Parc de la Ciutadella** ㉒ the city's largest park (daily 10am–sunset; free), which incorporates the zoo, the **Parc Zoológic** (www.zoobarcelona.cat; daily Oct–Mar 10am–5.30pm, Apr–May till 7pm, Jun–Sept till 8pm). This was the site, first, of the fortress built after the fall of Barcelona in 1714, and then of the 1888 World Exposition. Housed in a splendid *modernista* building designed for this event is the Laboratori de Natura, a branch of the Natural Science Museum (http://museuciencies.cat/en/) now housing its library and research centre. Nearby stands the Museu Martorell, which used to house the geological collection. Now it's yet another branch of the Natural Science Museum, which features the fully renovated 'Land of Dragons' which recreates the natural habitat of the komodo dragon and allows for panoramic views of the various levels of the enclosure.

Parc de la Ciutadella

The popular park is always a relaxing refuge from the intensity of the city's streets. It's a lovely place, with a lake where rowing boats can be hired, and shady benches beneath towering trees where parakeets have taken control. The large baroque fountain, **La Cascada**, was designed by Josep Fontseré, whose assistant was a young architecture student named Antoni Gaudí. In the Plaça d'Armes is the Parlament de Catalunya. The autonomous government debates the issues of the day in a handsome building, once the arsenal of the 18th-century citadel.

From the park's exit on Pujades a broad promenade sweeps up to the imposing **Arc de Triomf**, built as the entrance to the 1888 Exposition. To the right, near university buildings on Wellington, a tram can be caught to Diagonal Mar. On the sea side of the park lies the grand Estació de França railway station, and along Avinguda Marquès de l'Argentera is **La Llotja**, a centre of Barcelona's trading activities for more than 600 years and former Stock Exchange. It is a handsome building with an attractive courtyard and a 14th-century Gothic hall.

Almost opposite is the splendid arcade of **Porxos Xifré**, a 19th-century complex that houses the **Restaurant 7 Portes** (http://7portes.com/en), a Barcelona institution (see page 110). If you head back towards the Rambla past the city's monumental

Correus (Post Office), along Passeig de Colom, you will pass the baroque splendour of the **Mare de Déu de la Mercè** church. It is best known because the sculpture of the Madonna on the dome can be seen for miles around and is something of a local landmark.

EL RAVAL

The district between La Rambla, the Ronda de Sant Antoni and Paral.lel is **El Raval**, where numerous buildings have been demolished to create urban spaces and new housing in the latest trendy zone. From La Rambla, take Carrer del Carme, then turn right up Carrer dels Àngels to reach the most conspicuous symbol of this neighbourhood's transformation: Richard Meier's **Museu d'Art Contemporani de Barcelona** ㉓ (MACBA; www.macba.es; Mon, Wed–Fri 11am–7.30pm, Sat 10am–9pm, Sun 10am–3pm), which is worth visiting for its architecture and the multicultural buzz in its square, where skateboarders, art lovers and locals all congregate. It has some fine abstract works and good temporary exhibitions.

'48 Portraits' by Gerhard Richter, MACBA

Next door is the ever-stimulating **Centre de Cultura Contemporània de Barcelona** (CCCB; www.cccb.org; Tue–Sun 11am–8pm), a striking renovation of an old poor house, the Casa de Caritat. In this

exciting space dance, music, film and other activities explore the urban experience.

Retrace your steps to Carrer del Carme and the Gothic complex of the **Antic Hospital de la Santa Creu** (Hospital of the Holy Cross), a hospital and refuge for pilgrims for a thousand years. Gaudí died here in 1926. The present structures were begun in 1401. Look for the frieze of 16th-century tiles on the life of St Paul in the entryway of the Institut d'Estudis Catalans. The courtyard is restful, with benches under orange trees ripe with fruit or fragrant with blossom. The Escola Massana Art School, the National Library of Catalonia, and the Institute for Catalan Studies are all housed here.

URBAN REGENERATION

Carrer Hospital is a busy commercial street catering primarily to the Arab and Asian families living in the area. On and around it are some trendy little shops and restaurants, although the narrow alleys are best avoided. Check out Rieva Baixa for vintage shops, and the recently created Rambla del Raval. Old housing was demolished to make way for it, and new blocks and a towering 5-star hotel are all part of the urban regeneration process that is attracting a bohemian crowd.

Around the corner is a Romanesque gem, the little church of **Sant Pau del Camp** (www.santpaudelcamp.info; Mon–Fri 9.30am–12.30pm, 3.30pm–6.30pm, Sat 9.30am–12.30pm; free). The simplicity of its 12th-century lines is an agreeable change from the extravagance of Barcelona's *modernisme* and the intricacies of Gothic architecture. It is believed to be the oldest church in the city. The lovely little cloister has curious, Arab-style arches.

MONTJUÏC

Montjuïc came into its own as the site of Barcelona's 1929 International Exhibition, and again for the 1992 Olympic Games. It has since been rejuvenated so its shady gardens, 210-metre (689ft) summit, panoramic views and outstanding complex of museums and sports facilities are more popular than ever. The Plaça d'Espanya is a good point to begin a visit to Montjuïc, as it has a metro and bus stop. If you'd rather the more scenic route you can take the cable car directly to the castle. Beside the square is a bullring built in 1899, now home to the **Arenas de Barcelona**, a shopping, cultural and recreational facility. A central avenue leads upwards to the vast **Palau Nacional**, which houses the Catalan art museum, MNAC, and past the **Font Màgica** ㉔ (Magic Fountain), which performs a *son et lumière* show (Mar Thu–Sat 8pm–9pm, Apr–May Thu–Sat 9–10pm, Jun–Sep Wed–Sun 9.30–10.30pm, Oct Thu–Sat 9–10, Dec–early Jan Thu–Sat 8pm–9pm). Nearby is the seminal **Pavelló Mies van der Rohe** (www.miesbcn.com; daily

The frescoed dome of the Palau Nacional

10am–8pm), built for the 1929 Exposition, dismantled, then rebuilt in 1986. The glass, stone and steel cube house is a wonder of cool Bauhaus forms.

Opposite is **Casaramona**, a magnificent *modernista* textile factory converted into the **CaixaForum** (https://obrasociallacaixa.org; daily 10am–8pm; free), the Fundació la Caixa's wonderful cultural centre, with a full programme of exhibitions and concerts.

CATALAN ART TREASURES

External elevators make the ascent to the domed Palau Nacional easier. This is the **Museu Nacional d'Art de Catalunya** ㉕ (MNAC; www.museunacional.cat; Tue–Sat 10am–8pm, 6pm in winter, Sun 10am–3pm), housing one of the world's finest collections of Romanesque art. Another building constructed for the 1929 Exposition, it holds 1,000 years of Catalan art, bringing together various collections under one roof, including part of the

Thyssen-Bornemisza collection, and the 19th- and 20th-century collection of the former Museu d'Art Modern de Catalunya. It also holds excellent temporary exhibitions.

Between the 9th and 13th centuries, over 2,000 Romanesque churches were built in Catalonia. Interiors were decorated with painted altar panels, carved wooden crosses, Madonnas of great purity and primitive sculptures of biblical episodes or rural life on the capitals of columns. At the start of the 20th century many works were saved from deteriorating in abandoned churches and are now housed in the museum. There are masterpieces in every room. The Gothic wing is excellent, too. Many of the paintings are retablos, screens with arched frames that stood behind chapel altars. Among the treasures are Lluís Dalmau's painting *Virgin of the Councillors* (1445); Jaume Ferrer II's altarpiece St Jerome; and a fine retable of St John the Baptist with saints Sebastian and Nicholas.

The 19th- and 20th-century collection includes works by Casas, Fortuny, Mir, Nonell and Rusiñol. Displays have been further enhanced with a collection of paintings from Barcelona-born Carmen Thyssen-Bornemisza.

Cable cars

A funicular from Avinguda del Paral.lel metro station runs to Avinguda de Miramar (near the Fundació Joan Miró), and links up with the Telefèric (daily 10am–9pm, shorter hours in winter), the cable car that gives a ride with a view up to the Castell de Montjuïc. Another cable car, the Transbordador Aéri, runs from Montjuïc right across the port to Barceloneta (Jun–Aug daily 10.30am–8pm, Sep–Oct daily 10.30am–7pm, Nov–Feb daily 11am–5.30pm, Mar–May 10.30am–7pm), stopping at the World Trade Center.

MUSEUMS AND MIRÓ

Up the hill is the **Museu d'Arqueologia de Catalunya** ㉖ (www. mac.cat; Tue–Sat 9.30am–7pm, Sun 10am–2.30pm). Among the exhibits, drawn mainly from prehistoric, Iberian, Greek and Roman sites in Catalonia, are reconstructions of tombs and life-like dioramas. Around another curve, within walking distance uphill, is the **Museu Etnològic** (Tue–Sat 10am–7pm, till 8pm on Sun), highlighting the native arts of Latin America.

Further up lie the Jardins de Laribal, and on the edge of them is the **Teatre Grec** amphitheatre, where the Festival Grec is held in summer. Steps from here lead to the simple and elegant **Fundació Joan Miró** ㉗ (www.fmirobcn.org; Tue–Sat 10am–6pm, till 8pm in summer, Sun 10am-3pm, until 6pm in summer, free guided tours offered the first Sunday of each month, 11am in English). This excellent museum was designed by the archi-tect Josep Lluís Sert to house a large collection of paintings, drawings, tapestries and sculpture by the Catalan surrealist, who died in 1983 at the age of 90. The exhibits follow Miró's artistic development from 1914 onwards. Flooded with natural light, they are seen at their best. In the grounds outside are a number of his sculptures. The collection is witty and bright with the unique language symbols associated with the artist.

The **Castell de Montjuïc** (daily Apr-Sep 10am–8pm, Oct-Mar 10am–6pm, free on Sun from 3pm), built in 1640, remained in use by the army, then as a prison until shortly before it was turned over to the city in 1960. The fort has sombre associations for the city: its cannons bombarded the popula-tion to crush rebellions in the 18th and 19th centuries, and it was the site of political executions. The **Jardí Botànic** (www. museuciencies.bcn.cat; daily Nov–Mar 10–5pm, Apr–May and Sep–Oct until 7pm, June–Aug until 8pm), between the Olympic Stadium and the castle, is a sustainable garden showcasing plants from across the Mediterranean.

The **Anella Olímpica** (Olympic Ring) spreads across the northern side of Montjuïc and can be reached by escalator from the Palau Nacional. The original 1929 Estadi Olímpic (Olympic stadium) was enlarged for the 1992 Games and further alterations made for the European Athletics Championships in 2010. It now houses a state-of-the

Miró sculpture outside the Fundació Joan Miró

art Open Camp (www.opencamp.info), where groups of 25 or more are able to experience the world's first sports theme park offering 25 experiences related to different disciplines that blend sports activities with digital technologies. Near the entrance to the stadium is **Museu Olímpic i de l'Esport** ㉘ (www.museu olimpicbcn.cat; Tue–Sat 10am–6pm, till 8pm in summer, Sun 10am–2.30), a must for sports enthusiasts.

Just beyond is the high-tech **Palau Sant Jordi** sports stadium, designed by Japanese architect Arata Isozaki. It can seat 17,000 under a 45 metre- (148ft) high roof. Towering over it all is the 188-meter (616ft) -high **Torre de Calatrava** communications tower.

POBLE ESPANYOL

Down the hill is the **Poble Espanyol** ㉙ (Spanish Village; www. poble-espanyol.com; Mon 9am–8pm, Tue–Thur, Fri 9am–3am,

Teatre Nacional de Catalunya

Sat 9am–4am, Sun 9am–midnight), a family attraction by day and a popular nightspot. Built for the 1929 Exposition, it's a composite of architecture representing Spain's varied regions, including replicas of houses, church towers, fountains, plazas and palaces arranged along a network of streets and squares. The entrance is through a gate of the walled city of Ávila. There is a flamenco show, restaurants, discos and demonstrations of regional crafts, including weaving, pottery and glass-blowing, which make it a good place to find well-made souvenirs.

THE DIAGONAL

The broad Avinguda Diagonal slices across Cerdà's grid from the coast to the hills linking up with the city ring roads. From Diagonal Mar a tram runs through **22@ district** ③⓪ with its cutting-edge architecture up to the busy Plaça de les Glòries Catalanes roundabout. Jean Nouvel's gherkin-like **Torre Agbar** illuminated at night by 4,500 glass panels, spectacularly marks the spot. It was meant to house a five-star Hyatt hotel, but the deal fell through in 2017. Nearby is the state-of-the-art **Museu del Disseny** (Design Museum, Tue–Sun 10am–8pm) which opened in 2015. It houses four museums formerly in the Palau Reial: the Museu de

Ceràmica, the Museu de les Arts Decoratives, the Museu Tèxtil i d'Indumentària and the Gabinet de les Arts Gràfiques. Nearby is Ricardo Bofill's neoclassical **Teatre Nacional de Catalunya** and Rafael Moneo's **L'Auditori**, a concert hall which now includes the **Museu de la Música** (http://w110.bcn.cat; Tue–Fri 10am–6pm, Thu until 9pm, Sat–Sun 10am–7pm).

PEDRALBES

Further up the Diagonal is the **Palau de Pedralbes**, a Güell-family estate converted into a royal residence in 1919. On the other side of the Diagonal is the Zona Universitària and **Camp Nou Stadium**, home of Barcelona's revered football club, Barça, with a museum which includes a tour (www.fcbarcelona.com; most of the year 9.30am–6.30 except for match days; check website for details).

At the top of Avinguda de Pedralbes is the atmospheric **Monestir de Pedralbes** ③ (Tue–Sun 10am–6.30pm; http://monestirpedralbes.bcn.cat). Founded in 1326 by Queen Elisenda de Montcada, whose tomb is in the superb Gothic church, it has a beautiful three-storey cloister.

The districts on the hillsides were once separate villages where residents of Barcelona spent summers and weekends. They've been absorbed over the years, but each preserves its own character. Pedralbes is patrician – expensive, residential villas with gardens – while Sarrià retains the feel of a small Catalan town and is very charming.

TIBIDABO

The first bright, clear morning or late afternoon of your visit, head for **Tibidabo** ㉜, the 512-metre (1,680ft) peak of the Collserola range, overlooking the city. The views are

El Sagrat Cor

breathtaking. The church of **El Sagrat Cor**, floodlit at night, built in the first half of the 20th century in neo-Romanesque and neo-Gothic style, and surmounted by a monumental figure of Christ, is one of the city's landmarks.

To reach the summit, take the FGC train from the Plaça de Catalunya to Avda Tibidabo. From here the **Tramvia Blau**, an old-fashioned blue wooden tram, runs every day during the summer (weekends only in winter; for details go to www.tmb. cat/en/tramvia-blau), taking you up to the funicular station, past grand villas. Don't miss the nearby **CosmoCaixa** (www. agenda.obrasocial.lacaixa.es/cosmocaixa-barcelona; daily 10am–8pm), a splendid science museum with a Planetarium that projects a 3D show using the latest technology. Nearby is Torre Bellesguard (officially known as Casa Figueras; Tue–Sun 10am–3pm; www.bellesguardgaudi.com) – Antonio Gaudí's most personal project. The residence with an impressive tower was designed in the Neo-Gothic style in 1900-1909; next to it are the ruins of a 500-year old medieval castle.

From Plaça del Dr Andreu the funicular lifts you through pine woods to the top, where you have a spectacular panorama of the city, the coast and the Pyrenees. Families flock to the famous, 1950s-style amusement park, the **Parc d'Atraccions** (www.tibi dabo.cat; opening hours vary so check the website). With over 25 attractions, many of the old favourites remain but there is now a new generation of rides to experience, too. Check out the Sky Walk, an area with some of the best views of Barcelona.

The **Parc de Collserola** is a huge, green swathe that makes a great escape from the city. Families come here at weekends and summer evenings to enjoy the fresh air. There are jogging and cycling tracks, nature trails, picnic spots and *merenderos*, where you barbecue your own food.

Another high spot is the **Torre de Collserola** communications tower (www.torredecollserola.com; same hours as Parc d'Atraccions), designed by Sir Norman Foster for the 1992 Barcelona Olympics. A chic transparent lift whisks you to the top for fabulous panoramic views.

EXCURSIONS

There's a great deal to detain you in Barcelona, but just beyond the city are several sites eminently worthy of day trips. These include the holy Catalan shrine of Montserrat, the relaxed and pretty town of Sitges for beaches and museums, and the cava wine country in the region of Penedès.

MONTSERRAT

Montserrat ③③ (www.montserratvisita.com), Catalonia's most important religious retreat and the shrine of Catalan nationhood, rises out of the rather featureless Llobregat plain 48km (30 miles) northwest of Barcelona. The view from its 1,241-metre (4,075ft) summit can encompass both the Pyrenees and Mallorca, and the monastery itself can be seen from afar, surrounded by the jagged ridges that give it its name – the Serrated Mountain.

The first hermitages on the mountain may have been established by those trying to escape the Moorish invasion. One was enlarged as a Benedictine monastery in the 11th century and a century later it became the repository for **La Moreneta**, the Black Madonna, a small, wooden image of a Virgin (darkened by candle smoke) holding the infant Jesus on her lap and a globe in her right hand. The figure is said to be a carving by St Luke, later hidden by St Peter. Ever since, pilgrims – from commoners to kings – have climbed the mountain to worship the Catalan patron saint. More than a million pilgrims and tourists visit the shrine each year.

The **monastery** was burned to the ground by Napoleon's soldiers in 1808, abandoned in 1835 when all convents were sequestered by the state, and rebuilt in 1874. During the Spanish Civil War, La Moreneta was secretly replaced by a copy; the original remained hidden during the dictatorship. Although Catalan culture was suppressed, monks here continued to say Mass in Catalan.

The site of the monastery is spectacular, tucked into folds of rock high above the plain. On the eve of the saint's day, 27 April, the monks hold an all-night vigil attended by huge crowds. La Moreneta looks down from a gold-and-glass case, above and to the right of the altar in the **basilica**, but the faithful can touch or kiss her right hand through an opening. Each day the Escolans, the oldest boys' choir in Europe, founded in the 13th century, fill the basilica with their pure voices (Mon–Fri 1pm and 6.45pm, Sun 11am–12pm, and 6.45pm, no

Montserrat's monastery, set high in the mountains

choir June–mid-Aug and 26 Dec–8 Jan). The monastery and its underground **museum** (daily 10am–5.30pm) contain many valuable works of art, including paintings by El Greco.

Montserrat is also a popular goal for cyclists and mountain climbers who ascend the spires of rock above the building. From the monastery there are walks to other hermitages and a funicular to the **Santa Cova**, the cave sacred to the legend of the Madonna. Statues and plaques line the paths. Due to its popularity, Montserrat has a number of bars, restaurants and shops around the Plaça de la Creu. For a peaceful visit, spend the night in the hotel or former monks' cells.

Getting There

Montserrat can be reached in an hour by FGC train from Barcelona's Plaça d'Espanya to either Montserrat Aeri, where a cable car continues up the side of the mountain to the

Sant Sebastià beach in Sitges

monastery, or the next stop, Monistrol de Montserrat, where the more comfortable Cremallera train travels up to the monastery, for the same price. If you are driving, leave Barcelona via the Diagonal and take the A2 highway in the direction of Lleida, taking the exit to Manresa for Monistrol.

SITGES

It's easy to get to the Costa Daurada beaches from Barcelona. The coast south of the city earned its name from its broad, golden sands, in contrast to the rocky coves of the Costa Brava to the north. **Sitges 34**, a favourite resort (www.visitsitges.com) of Barceloneses, is the best place for a day trip. It's a short drive on the R2 motorway, or a 40-minute train ride from Sants or Passeig de Gràcia stations, if you get a fast train – some of them stop frequently en route. There is also a scenic coastal drive which is narrow and curvy and obviously takes longer.

Happily, the pretty little town has escaped the high-rises and tawdry atmosphere of many coastal resorts, although it does get somewhat overwhelmed by crowds in summer. There are two beaches, separated by a promontory where gleaming, whitewashed houses cluster around the church of **Sant Bartolomeu i Santa Tecla**. The biggest and best beach is **Platja d'Or** (Golden Beach), backed by a palm-lined promenade and dozens of cafés and restaurants – some of them very good indeed. North of the promontory is Sant Sebastià beach, smaller, quieter and extremely pleasant.

Three Seaside Museums

Besides the beaches, Sitges is known for its appealing museums. The **Museu Cau Ferrat** (Tue–Sun July–Sept 10am–8pm, Nov–Mar 10am–5pm, Apr–June and Oct 10am–7pm http://museusdesitges. cat) is in the house built by the painter Santiago Rusiñol (1861–1931), whose collection of works by El Greco, Casas, Picasso and others is on display, along with many of his own works.

Next to Cau Ferrat is the **Museu Maricel** (Tue–Sun July–Sept 10am–8pm, Nov–Mar 10am–5pm, Apr–June, Oct 10am–7pm), a splendid house overlooking the sea – the name means 'sea and sky'. It displays a small collection of Gothic sculpture and paintings, some notable murals by Josep Maria Sert (1876–1945) and the town's art collection, with paintings by the Romantics, Lumanists and Modernists.

The nearby **Museu Romàntic** (during its ongoing renovations it is best to check the opening hours before visiting.), on Sant Gaudenci, displays the furniture and accoutrements of a wealthy 19th-century family, as well as a large collection of antique dolls, the Lola Anglada collection.

On the outskirts of Sitges are the villas of wealthy Barceloneses, while the pretty streets between the beach and station are geared for food and fun. Sitges has one of Spain's largest gay communities, and attracts gay travellers year-round, but particularly during the riotous February carnival. Gay and nudist beaches lie a little way beyond the other beaches of the town.

Located inland from Sitges, on the road to Vilafranca, is **Sant Pere de Ribes**, which has a 10th-century castle and a delightful Romanesque church.

SANT SADURNÍ D'ANOIA (PENEDÈS)

Cava, Catalonia's sparkling wine, comes from the **Penedès**, a pretty region south of Barcelona (about 45 minutes on the train from Sants or Plaça de Catalunya stations; by road, take the AP7 in the direction of Tarragona). These days the top-selling cavas are produced by Codorníu and Freixenet. The centre of cava production is the small town of **Sant Sadurní d'Anoia** 35, where several wineries offer guided tours and tastings.

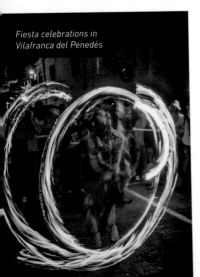

Fiesta celebrations in Vilafranca del Penedès

The most interesting of these is **Codorníu** (www.codorniu.com; tel: 90-209-0625 to check opening times and arrange a visit). This is Spain's largest producer of cava and has been in the business since 1872. The family-owned winery is located on a spectacular campus, with *modernista* buildings by Gaudí's contemporary, Puig i Cadafalch. Completed in 1898, it has been declared a National Artistic and Historic Monument. Visitors to the winery are taken on a theme-park-like ride through 26km (16 miles) of atmospheric underground cellars.

World-famous cava producer **Freixenet** has its headquarters next to the station (www.freixenet.es; tel: 93-891 7096; Mon–Sat 10am–6pm, Sun 9am–3pm, with exceptions).

There are some good restaurants in and near town, which the staff at Codorníu will be happy to tell you about. Most of them specialise in seafood accompanied, of course, by cava. If you visit the area between January and March you must try another regional dish, *calçots* – baby leeks grilled and dipped in a peppery, garlicky sauce – so popular they actually have a fiesta in their honour at this time, called the *calçotada*.

VILAFRANCA DEL PENEDÈS

Some 15km (8 miles) to the south of Sant Sadurní, surrounded by vineyards, is the town of **Vilafranca del Penedès** ③, the capital of the Alt-Penedès region and the place where the world-renowned Torres red wine is produced.

The **Vinseum: Museu de les Cultures del Vi de Catalunya** (www.vinseum.cat; May–Sept Tue–Sat 10am–7pm, Sun 10am–2pm, rest of the year Tue–Sat 10am–2pm and 4–7pm, Sun 10am–2pm) is said to be one of the best wine museums in Europe. It is housed in the renovated Gothic **Palau Reial**, residence of the count-kings of Barcelona-Aragón. The local festival (29 August–2 September), when the wine flows freely and the human towers called *castells* make their appearance, is a good time to visit the town and a great way to round off your holiday.

The extravagant Grand Teatre del
Liceu opera house

WHAT TO DO

SHOPPING

Barcelona is firmly on the map of European shopping capitals. As a city of eminent style and taste, it is packed full of fashion boutiques from high-street brands to top designers, antique shops, state-of-the-art home interior stores and art galleries. Design is taken very seriously here. Catalonia still thrives on family-owned shops, and window shopping on the Rambla de Catalunya or Passeig de Gràcia is a delight. The best items include fashionable clothing, shoes and leather products, antiques, books, high-tech design, home furnishings, objets d'art and music.

WHERE TO LOOK

Passeig de Gràcia, Rambla de Catalunya and **Diagonal** are great for fashion, jewellery, design and art galleries. Alternative fashion shops, galleries and street markets are dotted around the **Barri Gòtic, El Born** and **El Raval**. Plaça de Catalunya is the jumping-off point for some of the best shopping streets: **Portal de l'Àngel, Pelai** and **Carrer Portaferrisa** are always swarming with shoppers. The upper section of La Rambla has some leading fashion stores, though tacky souvenir shops are rife.

DEPARTMENT STORES AND MALLS

The major department store is **El Corte Inglés** (www.elcorte ingles.es), Spain's biggest. There is the huge, original branch on Plaça de Catalunya, one in Portal de l'Àngel, and one in the Diagonal (all open 9.30am–9pm). Also in Plaça de Catalunya is a large complex called **El Triangle** (Mon–Sat 9.30am-9pm; www.eltriangle.es), which includes perfume emporium Sephora and

FNAC, which has the city's best selection of national and foreign music, magazines, books, DVDs and the very latest in computer wizardry. **L'Illa** (www.lilla.com), on the Diagonal (above Plaça Francesc Macià), is one of Barcelona's best upmarket shopping malls. In **Port Vell** the Maremàgnum (www.maremagnum.es) mall is teeming with shops and open 10am–10pm, including Sundays. One of the largest and best equipped malls is **Diagonal Mar** (www.diagonalmarcentre.es) by the sea near the Forum, easily reached by metro, it also contains an international cinema. Barcelona's newest and most spectacular mall, **Las Arenas** (www.arenasde barcelona.com), is in Montjuïc.

ANTIQUES AND ART GALLERIES

Some of the best spots for antiques are in the old town, along **Banys Nous, de la Palla,** and **Baixada Santa Eulàlia,** between the cathedral and the Plaça del Pi. An antiques market is held every Thursday in the cathedral square. There are several individual shops around the Eixample, and **Bulevar dels Antiquaris**, at Passeig de Gràcia 57, conceals a maze of dealers.

For art purchases, explore **Consell de Cent**, in the Eixample; the **Born**, a hot gallery-browsing area; and the streets around the contemporary art museum, MACBA, in **El Raval**. There are several galleries on **Petritxol,** near Plaça del Pi, and **Montcada,** clustered around the Museu Picasso. Ceramics, ranging from traditional tiles, plates and bowls with brightly coloured glazing, to more modern creations, can be found in the streets around the cathedral and along **Montcada**. A selection of good-quality ceramics and handicrafts is sold at Art Escudellers (Escudellers 23–25). BCN Original, next to the tourist information office at Plaça de Catalunya 17, has a good selection of specifically-designed gifts that are too nice to call 'souvenirs'. Many museum shops also sell high-quality art and design items.

BOOKS

Spain's publishing industry is based in Barcelona, so it's easy to find a wide assortment of books, including many titles in English. Excellent glossy books on Spanish culture, art and cookery and lots of discounted titles – many in English – are found at Come In (www.libreriainglesa.com), an English bookshop at Balmes and Rosselló while La Central (http://www.lacentral.com) in Elisabets is a haven for browsers, located in a for-mer chapel. Laie (www.laie.es) on Pau Claris is an excellent bookshop-cum-café/restaurant. It also has branches in the CCCB (Contemporary Culture Centre) and other muse-ums throughout the city. Hibernian Books (www.hibernian-books.com) in Gràcia (Carrer Montseny) has a wide range of sec-ond-hand English books.

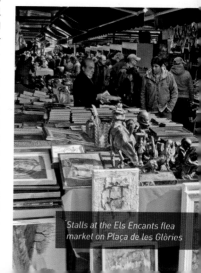
Stalls at the Els Encants flea market on Plaça de les Glòries

DESIGN

For quintessential Catalan and international design, Passage Barcelona (Abat Samsó 7; http://passagebcn.com), Barcelona's trendy design emporium, is full of funky furniture, unconventional art, timeless fashion and Karl Lagerfeld accessories – a great place to wander and get inspired. It also hosts art exhibitions and has a champagne bar. Pilma (Diagonal 403; https://es.pilma.com) has good stock and low-key good taste, but less innate style; the Born area is good for trendy, original items.

FASHION

Cool fashion for men and women by Toni Miró can be found at his signature store (Antoni Miró; www.antoniomiro.es) at Calle Enric Granados 46. Galician designer Adolfo Domínguez sells classic fashion at Passeig de Gràcia 32, Plaza de Catalunya 14 and Diagonal 617. Loewe in Casa Lleó Morera (Passeig de Gràcia 35) is Spain's premier leather goods store. An iconic Catalan name in fashion is the dynamic Custo-Barcelona, whose stores can be found in several locations across town including La Rambla 109.

Markets

Barcelona's biggest and best flea market is Els Encants, which pulsates with action every Monday, Wednesday, Friday and Saturday 9am–7/8pm near Plaça de les Glòries Catalanes (Glòries metro). Some of the stuff is good, some is rubbish, but it's all good fun. For stamps, coins, and memorabilia, go to the Plaça Reial on Sunday morning, or to the Sant Antoni market for records and books. Plaça Sant Josep Oriol has a weekend art fair and there is an antiques fair every Thursday (in summer) in the cathedral square.

FOOD

Colmado Quílez (Rambla de Catalunya 63; https://

lafuente.es) is a classic Catalan grocery, with packaged goods, fine wines, cheeses, and imported beer in a photogenic corner shop. Since 1851, the place to find roasted nuts, dried fruits, coffee and spices, has been Casa Gispert (Sombrerers 23; www.casagispert.com) near Santa Maria del Mar. Escribà (www.escriba. es), at La Rambla 83, is a beautiful shop, more than a century-old, selling wonderful chocolates. For a religious experience and a history lesson with your shopping, visit Caelum (de la Palla 8; www.caelumbarcelona.com), which stocks a variety of products produced by Trappist monks, such as beers, honey, candles and cheese plus a delicious assortment of tea and pastries. Downstairs is a cellar/tea room where the ancient foundations of 14th-century women's baths were uncovered and are open to the public.

La Boqueria - the best place for fresh produce

The ultimate food shopping experience in Barcelona, of course, is Mercat La Boqueria (www.boqueria.info; see page 28) for fish, meat, fruit, vegetables, charcuterie and olives. It's open Monday to Saturday till 8pm and it's not to be missed.

ENTERTAINMENT

While Barcelona may not be quite as fanatical about late nights as Madrid, it is still a place that really comes to life when the sun goes down. It has virtually every kind of entertainment, from cool cabarets to live jazz, rock to flamenco and world music, opera, symphony concerts, dynamic theatre and dance and a thriving bar and club scene. At night, some streets, such as La Rambla, become slow-moving rivers of people just walking and talking. The main churches and monuments are illuminated, and the city takes on a new and stimulating aspect.

MUSIC, BALLET AND THEATRE

A concert at the **Palau de la Música** (Carrer del Palau de la Música 4–6; tel: 93-295 7200; www.palaumusica.cat), the *modernista* masterpiece, is a wonderful experience, whatever the performance is. The varied programme includes chamber and symphony concerts, contemporary music and occasionally jazz.

Barcelona's famous opera house, **Gran Teatre del Liceu** (La Rambla 51–59; tel: 93-485 99 00; www.liceubarcelona.cat), which was gutted by fire in 1994, reopened to general acclaim in 1999. It hosts extravagant and avant-garde productions and a short ballet season. Tickets are hard to get, despite its increased seating capacity, but worth a try. **L'Auditori** (Plaça de les Arts), home of the OBC (Barcelona Symphony Orchestra), has a 2,500-seat auditorium and a smaller one for chamber concerts (for tickets tel: 93-247 9300; www.auditori.cat).

The **CaixaForum** (Av. de Francesc Ferrer I Guàrdia 6-8; tel: 93-476 8600) is a sophisticated cultural centre that hosts musical performances as well as exhibitions and other events.

For theatre, there is the **Teatre Nacional de Catalunya** (Plaça de les Arts; tel: 93-306 5720; www.tnc.cat), with a wide and varied programme, and the **Teatre Lliure** (Passeig de Santa Madrona; tel: 93-238 7625; www.teatrelliure.com) for good contemporary productions. Most productions are in Catalan, occasionally Spanish, and foreign companies visit at festival time. The **Mercat de les Flors** (Lleida 59; tel: 93-256 2600; http://mer catflors.cat) specialises in dance and movement.

Tickets for cultural events can be booked at the information centre in Palau Virreina on La Rambla (Tue–Sun 11am–8pm) and at the venue's box office.

FLAMENCO AND JAZZ

Flamenco is not a Catalan tradition, but some *tablaos* – live flamenco perfor-

Harlem Jazz Club

mances – are staged for tourists. Tablao Flamenco Cordobés (La Rambla 35; tel: 93-317 5711; www.tablaocordobes.com) is the most popular, while El Patio Andaluz (Rocafort, 231; tel: 93-209 3378; www.showflamencobarcelona.com) also puts on *sevillanas*, traditional Andalusian music. There are also daily shows at El Tablao de Carmen in the Poble Espanyol on Montjuïc (Avda. Francesc Ferrer i Guàrdia 13; tel: 93-325 6895; www.tablaodecar men.com). One of the most authentic shows is at Los Tarantos in Plaça Reial (tel: 93-319 1789; www.masimas.com/tarantos).

Live jazz can be found most nights at Harlem Jazz Club in the Gothic Quarter (Comtessa de Sobradiel 8; www.har lemjazzclub.es), fused with world music and flamenco. Jamboree (www.masimas.com/jamboree), in the Plaça Reial, is also good. Luz de Gas (Muntaner 246; www.luzdegas.com) presents jazz, rock and soul, and becomes a dance venue after midnight.

NIGHTLIFE

For seasoned *juerguistas* (ravers) the Barcelona nightlife is hard to beat. From sundown to sunrise there's a venue for every taste and the streets buzz as if it were midday. For early evening don't miss atmospheric cocktail bars **Boadas** (Tallers 1), famed for its mojitos, and long-established **Dry Martini** (Aribau 162), or a terrace bar in a square in the Gràcia neighbourhood, where a young, laid-back crowd gather.

The scene really hots up after midnight, much of it centred on the Old Town, where a few remnants of the old Barri Xino mingle with hip new nightspots and restaurants like Iposa (Floristes de la Rambla, 14) that are open for drinks well past midnight. The Born area is still cool for classics like **Gimlet** (Santaló 46) or **Berimbau** (Passeig del Born 17), while the Plaça Reial in the Gothic Quarter has every kind of nightspot from disco **Karma** (www.karmadisco. com) to **Sidecar** (www.sidecarfactoryclub.com) with its live gigs. Uptown, some of the original 1980s designer bars and clubs are still going strong, such as **Otto Zutz** (Lincoln 15; www.ottozutz. com) with its three dance floors, and **Ommsession**, hip hotel Omm's club (Rosselló 265; www.hotelomm.com). New on the scene, **Bling Bling** (Carrer de Tuset 10; http://blingblingbcn.com) is a very chic, upmarket club challenging these old favourites, and **Sala Apolo** (Nou de la Rambla 113; www.sala-apolo.com) and **Razzmatazz** (Pamplona 88; www.salarazzmatazz.

Listings magazines

The cultural guide *Guía del Ocio* (available online at http://enbarcelona.com in Spanish) has up-to-date entertainment information, while the *Metropolitan*, a free monthly English magazine, has listings, reviews and articles (www. barcelona-metropolitan. com). Their website lists where to find copies.

com) are two of the coolest spots in town. Halfway up Tibidabo is **Mirablau** (Plaça del Dr Andreu 2; www. mirablaubcn.com), a bar-club with a panoramic view of the city. Irresistible in the summer are the beach bars or *chiringuitos* on every beach from Barceloneta to Diagonal Mar, where you can dance in the sand till dawn.

Human castles at La Mercè Festival

FESTIVALS

There are numerous music festivals: the **Festival de Guitarra de Barcelona** (www.theproject.es) in March, the **Festival Internacional de Jazz** (www.jazz.barcelona) in October and November, and the **Grec Summer Festival** of dance, music and theatre (http://lameva.barcelona.cat/grec/en) in July. Events are held all over the city, but the most impressive are at the **Grec Theatre**, an open air amphitheatre on Montjuïc (check programme and buy tickets at the Virreina Palace, La Rambla 99; see page 27).

If you're in the city during a festival you'll see the different neighbourhoods erupt into life. Food, fireworks, music and the huge papier-mâché effigies called *gegants* (giants) and their companions, the *cap grossos* (bigheads), are essential features. The *gegants* are about 4 metres (13ft) high and elaborately dressed as kings and queens, knights and ladies. *Cap grossos* are cartoon heads of well-known personalities, often accompanied by *dracs* (dragons) and *dimonis* (devils).

A constant of Catalan festivals are the *castellers*, acrobatic troupes of men, boys and girls who form human towers up to nine men high. This takes place most spectacularly at the **La Mercè Festival**, the city's patron saint, on 24 September (festivities begin a few days before), in the Plaça de Sant Jaume. The **pre-Lent Carnaval** is another good excuse to dress up and hold processions and parties. Like most festivals it is accompanied by late-night bands and plenty of fireworks (see page 96 for major events).

SPORTS

The 1992 Olympics cemented Barcelona's reputation as a sports-mad city. Barceloneses are wild about Barça, their championship football (soccer) club, and are avid spectators of basketball, tennis, handball, golf and motorsport. But they're also active sports enthusiasts, eager to escape the city for cycling, sailing or skiing, the latter only a couple of hours away in the Pyrenees.

SPECTATOR SPORTS

The great spectator sport in Barcelona is football, and a match involving Barça (www.fcbarcelona.com), one of Europe's perennial champions, can bring the city to a standstill. The club's **Camp Nou** stadium, in the Les Corts area near the Diagonal, is the largest in Europe. Camp Nou has one of the most visited museums in Spain (check website for details). Match tickets can be purchased ahead online at the club's website or on the day at the ticket office on Travessera de les Corts, but tickets can be scarce for big matches. The city does have another football club, Espanyol, who are based at the **RCDE stadium** in the suburb of Cornella de Llobregat; match tickets for their games are easier to get hold of (www.rcdespanyol.com).

The city's second favourite spectator sport is basketball. FC Barcelona Bàsquet (www.fcbarcelona.com) play at the **Palau Blaugrana**, on the same site as Camp Nou. They share the facilities with the roller hockey, *futsal* (indoor football) and handball teams. The season runs from September to May and tickets can be purchased directly at Palau Blaugrana or online.

Barça fans at the Camp Nou stadium

Tennis is also popular, and the prestigious **Real Club de Tennis Barcelona-1899** (www.rctb1899.es) off Av. Diagonal near Pedralbes, with seating for some 8400 spectators, stages the Barcelona Open APT World Tour tournament each April.

PARTICIPANT SPORTS

Recreational cycling and jogging on Montjuïc and Tibidabo is very popular, and of course swimming – whether at the city beaches or along the Costa Daurada and Costa Brava – is a prime activity. Visitors can hire skates or bikes, play golf at one of the fine courses near the city, or visit Tibidabo's **Can Caralleu sports centre** (tel: 93-203 7874; www.claror.cat/cancaralleu), which has tennis, *pelota*, volleyball and two swimming pools.

Cycling is popular and tourist offices can provide a map showing recommended routes and bike lanes and advice about taking bikes on public transport. Or contact **Amics de**

Inhabitant of the Parc Zoológic

la Bici (Demóstenes 19; tel: 93-339 4060; www. amicsdelabici.org). On Tibidabo, the **Carretera de las Aiguas**, a path that winds along the mountain with spectacular views of the city below, is a great place to walk, jog or cycle. **Barcelona by Bike** offers easy-going tours around the city (tel: 671 307 325; www.barcelonabybike. com). Bikes can be rented from **Biciclot** (Pere IV, 58; tel: 93-307 7475; www.bici clot.coop), where there is easy access to the Parc de la Ciutadella and the waterfront (tandems and child seats available).

At the **Reial Club de Golf El Prat** (El Prat de Llobregat; tel: 93-728 1000; www.realclubdegolfelprat.com), offers 45 holes designed by golfing legend Greg Norman. Clubs and carts can be hired, and there's a pool for non-participants. Other courses located nearby include **Club de Golf Sant Cugat** (Sant Cugat del Vallès; tel: 93-674 3908; www.golfsantcugat.com), just west of the city, which hires out clubs and trolleys and has a pool; and the **Terramar course** at Sitges (tel: 93-894 0580; http://golfter ramar.com). For additional information, visit www.catgolf.com.

For sailing information, you can contact the **Reial Club Marítim** (tel: 93-221 4859; www.maritimbarcelona.org). For watersports and equipment hire in general, try **Base Nautica de la Mar Bella** on Platja Mar Bella, Av. Litoral (tel: 93-221 0432; http://basenautica.org).

Skiing in the Pyrenees is popular. Most resorts are within two hours of Barcelona; some are accessible by train, and there are cheap weekend excursions available. Information can be obtained from the **Asociació Catalana d'Estacions d'Esquí** (tel: 93-416 0194; www.catneu.cat).

CHILDREN

Barcelona is an excellent city for children. Taking young children to restaurants is a regular occurrence, so they are completely accepted. The clean beaches will keep most children and parents happy in between sightseeing, and the Port Vell waterfront has **L'Aquàrium** (Moll d'Espanya; tel: 93-221 7474; www.aquariumbcn. com), one of the largest aquariums in Europe. The **Zoo** (Ciutadella Park; www.zoobarcelona.cat), hosts lions and tigers and bears along with numerous other species, while the park itself, with boats for hire, is fun and shady. The **Poble Espanyol** (Montjuïc; www.poble-espanyol.com), a recreation of a Spanish village, is popular with families, both locals and visitors, and manages to interest teenagers as well as children (see page 71).

Tibidabo amusement park (Parc d'Atraccions; tel: 93-211 7942; www.tibidabo.cat) is good family fun, and kids love to arrive there on the Tramvia Blau (see page 74). As for museums, the science museum **CosmoCaixa** below the park is full of child-friendly exhibits, including an area dedicated to three- to six-year-olds (see page 74). The **Museu de la Xocolata** (Chocolate Museum; Antic Convent de Sant Agustí, La Ribera; www.museuxocolata. cat) has tempting chocolate sculptures, while the **Museu de Cera** (Wax Museum; www.museocerabcn.com) with its lifelike models, is usually a hit as well. Teenagers can spend hours watching skateboarders in front of the MACBA (Plaça dels Angels) or joining in themselves.

CALENDAR OF EVENTS

5 January Reis Mags (Three Kings' Day). Gift giving and procession.

February (second week) Feast of Santa Eulàlia, a winter *Festa Major* that's a low-key version of La Mercè (see 24 September).

February–March Carnival, preceding Lent, is a wild celebration. Sitges carnival is the best in the region.

Setmana Santa/Easter Palm Sunday processions and services on Holy Thursday/Good Friday.

23 April Feast of Sant Jordi (St George). Book and rose stalls are set up in La Rambla and Passeig de Gràcia.

27 April Feast of Virgin of Montserrat. Liturgical rituals, choir singing and sardana dancing.

11 May Sant Ponç. Herb fair in Carrer de l'Hospital.

Mid-June Corpus Christi. Carpets of flowers and processions in Sitges. In Barcelona 'dancing eggs' are balanced on the spray of the cathedral fountain and fountains in other courtyards in the Barri Gòtic.

23–24 June Sant Joan (St John). A major event in Catalonia, with fireworks, feasting and flowing cava.

July Grec Summer Festival of theatre, dance, classical, pop and rock music.

15–21 August Festa Major de Gràcia. Street parties, parades, fireworks and concerts in Gràcia neighbourhood.

11 September Diada. Catalan national day, with demonstrations and flag waving.

24 September La Mercè. Barcelona's week-long festival, in honour of its patron, Mare del Déu de la Mercè (Our Lady of Mercy). Fireworks, music and dancing in the streets. Head to Plaça St Jaume to see *castells*; the Ball de Gegants is a parade of huge papier-mâché figures; Correfoc is a rowdy nocturnal parade of devils and fire-spitting dragons, not to be missed.

1–23 December Santa Llúcia Fair selling Nativity figurines, art, crafts and Christmas trees in front of the cathedral.

26 December Sant Esteve (St Stephen's Day). Families meet for an even larger meal than that eaten on Christmas Day.

EATING OUT

Catalans adore eating, and especially love dining out, the epitome of social activity. They enjoy one of the finest, most imaginative cuisines in Spain, and Barcelona is the best place to sample its rich variety. The cooking is an attractive mix of haute cuisine and the traditional rustic cooking that has fed Catalans for centuries.

Barcelona's restaurants begin with a major advantage: superb ingredients, as anyone who's entered a great covered market in the city can attest. Catalan cooking is based on *cuina del mercat* – market cuisine. Fresh fish and shellfish lead the menus (even though they're often flown in from the north coast and Galicia), and fruits and vegetables are at their freshest. Mountain-cured hams and spicy sausages, spit-roasted meats and fowl with aromatic herbs are specialities. Expect *all i oli* (garlic and olive oil mayonnaise), produce from the countryside, and wild mushrooms – *bolets* – an object of obsession for people from all over Catalonia.

Barcelona's cosmopolitan population enjoys food from every Spanish region; Basque cookery is especially appreciated and Basque tapas bars have sprouted like the much-loved wild mushrooms.

Freshly prepared tapas

An evening at Mercat de la Boqueria

International cuisine used to mean French, but the number of restaurants from all over the world has exploded. Most top restaurants are in the Old Town and the Eixample, though the most lively areas are along the waterfront, in the new port and in El Born. The most exclusive restaurants tend to be in the *Barrios Altos*, uptown residential neighbourhoods. Eating out in Barcelona is a treat and can be one of the highlights of your trip. Restaurants are not cheap, but they compare favourably with those in many European and North American capitals. Sometimes menus are offered only in Catalan, so always ask if there is one in English or Castilian Spanish.

MEAL TIMES AND MENUS

Barceloneses, like all Spaniards, eat late. Lunch usually isn't eaten until 2 or 3pm. Dinner is served from about 9pm until 11.30pm, although at weekends people sometimes don't sit down to dinner until midnight. You can usually get a meal at almost any time of the day, but if you enter a restaurant soon after the doors have swung open, you are likely to find yourself dining alone, or with other foreign visitors. You could always adopt the Spanish system, which is to pace yourself for the late hours by eating tapas.

Barceloneses tend to eat a three-course meal at lunchtime, including dessert and coffee. Nearly all restaurants offer a lunchtime *menú del día* or *menú de la casa*, a daily set menu that is a really good bargain. For a fixed price you'll get three courses: a starter, often soup or salad, a main dish, and dessert (ice-cream, a piece of fruit or the ubiquitous *flan*, a kind of caramel custard), plus wine, beer or bottled water, and bread. Typically, the cost is about half what you'd expect to pay if you ordered from the regular menu. The idea is for people to be able to eat economically near their workplace, though many travel home in the two-hour lunch break. It's not uncommon to share a first course, or to order *un sólo plato* – just a main course.

You can also eat cheaply in *cafeterías*, where you will usually be offered *a plat combinat (plato combinado* in Castilian Spanish), usually meat or fish with chips and salad, served on the same plate. Not the best way to eat, but fast and inexpensive.

Reservations are recommended at Barcelona's more popular restaurants, especially from Thursday to Saturday. Many are closed on Sunday night. Prices generally include

⊙ TAPAS

Tapas – the snacks for which Spanish bars and cafés are world-famous – come in dozens of delicious varieties, from appetisers such as olives and salted almonds, to vegetable salads, fried squid, garlicky shrimps, lobster mayonnaise, meatballs, spiced potatoes, wedges of omelette, sliced sausage and cheese. The list is virtually endless, and can be surprisingly creative, especially at the now extremely popular Basque tapas joints.

A dish larger than a tapa is called a *porción*. A large serving, meant to be shared, is a *ración*, and half of this, a media *ración*. Best of all, tapas are usually available throughout the day, and are a great way to try new flavours.

service, but it's customary to leave a small tip, usually under 10 percent.

Your choices are not limited to restaurants and *cafeterías*. Most bars (also called *tabernas*, *bodegas* and *cervecerías*) serve food, often of a surprisingly high standard. Here you can have a selection of tapas, sandwiches (*bocadillos* in Spanish, *bocats* or *entrepans* in Catalan) or limited *plats combinats* at almost any time of the day.

Breakfast is a trivial affair in most of Spain, Barcelona included, except at hotels that offer mega-buffets as money-makers or enticements. (Check to see if breakfast is included in the room price at your hotel; if not, it's probably better to try the nearest café or *cafetería*.) Local people usually have a coffee accompanied by bread, toast, a pastry or croissant. The occasional bar and *cafetería* may serve an 'English breakfast' of bacon and eggs.

LOCAL SPECIALITIES

The foundation of rustic Catalan cuisine is *pa amb tomàquet* – slices of rustic bread rubbed with garlic and halves of beautifully fresh tomatoes, doused with olive oil, and sprinkled with coarse salt. Another typical Catalan dish is *espinacs a la catalana*, spinach prepared with pine nuts, raisins and garlic. Others include *escudella* (a thick tasty Catalan soup); *suquet de peix* (fish and shellfish soup); *fuet* (long, salami-type sausage); and *fideus* (long, thin noodles served with pork, sausage and red pepper). A popular local fish served in a variety of ways is *rape* (angler fish), especially tasty prepared *a l'all cremat* (with roasted garlic). Other good bets are *llobina al forn* (baked sea bass) and *llenguado a la planxa* (grilled sole). You might be fooled by the Catalan word for a Spanish *tortilla* (omelette), which is *truita*, but translates as both omelette and trout. *Bacallà*, the lowly salt cod, is now served in the most distinguished restaurants in various guises and is not cheap. A *sarsuela* is a stew of fish cooked in its own juices; a *graellada de peix* is a mixed grill of fish.

Other specialities are *llebre estofada amb xocolata* (stewed hare in a bitter-sweet chocolate sauce). Barcelona's all-purpose sausage is the hearty *botifarra*, often served (in spring) with *faves a la catalana* (young broad beans stewed with bacon, onion and garlic in an earthen-

Pa amb tomàquet topped with anchovies

ware casserole). *Xató* (pronounced *sha-toe*) is the endive and olive salad of Sitges, fortified with tuna or cod, and has an especially good sauce made of red pepper, anchovies, garlic and ground almonds. The word for salad of any kind is *amanida*.

Although it originates in rice-growing Valencia, the classic seafood paella is high on many visitors' lists of dishes to sample in Barcelona. Try the restaurants in Barceloneta for a paella of fresh mussels, clams, shrimp and several kinds of fish. It will take about 20 minutes to prepare. Avoid the ready-made paellas flouted by tourist-trap restaurants, especially on La Rambla.

When it comes to dessert, *flan* is ubiquitous, but there's a home-made version, the more liquid *crema catalana* (egg custard with caramelised sugar on top). If they say it's *casera* (home-made) then don't hesitate. *Mel i mato* is a treat made with honey and creamy cheese. The best sweet things are the delightful delicacies sold in pastry shops.

Dry Martini cocktail bar

DRINKS

In addition to an assortment of fine wines from across Spain, Barcelona presents an opportunity to try some excellent regional wines. Penedès, the grape-growing region just outside Barcelona, produces some excellent wines, including *cava*, which goes well with seafood and most tapas. Among Penedès reds, try Torres Gran Coronas, Raimat and Jean León. Wines from the Priorat area are superb, expensive reds that rival the best in Spain. White wines from the La Rueda region are generally good.

Sangría is a favourite, made of wine and fruit, fortified with brandy, but it's drunk more by visitors than locals. Spanish beers, available in bottles and on draft, are generally light and refreshing. A glass of draught beer is a *caña*.

You'll find every kind of sherry (*jerez*) here. The pale, dry *fino* is sometimes drunk not only as an apéritif but also with soup and fish courses. Rich dark *oloroso* goes well after dinner. Spanish brandy varies from excellent to rough: you usually get what you pay for. It is advisable to request a particular brand when asking for spirits.

Coffee is served black (*solo/sol*), with a spot of milk (*cortado/tallat*), or half and half with hot milk (*con leche/amb llet*). *Horchata de chufa*, made with ground tiger nuts, is popular in summer, and is sold in bars called *horchaterías* which also sell ice cream.

TO HELP YOU ORDER

Could we have a table, please? **¿Nos puede dar una mesa, por favor?**

Do you have a set menu? **¿Tiene un menú del día?**

I'd like a/an/some… **Quisiera…**

The bill, please **La cuenta, por favor**

MENU READER

a la plancha grilled
agua water
al ajillo in garlic
arroz rice
asado roasted
atún tuna
azúcar sugar
bacalao dried salt cod
bocadillo sandwich
calamares squid
cangrejo crab
caracoles snails
la carne de cerdo pork
la carne de vaca beef
cerveza beer
champiñones mushrooms
chorizo spicy sausage
cordero lamb
croquetas croquettes
ensalada salad
filete steak
flan caramel custard
gambas prawns
gazpacho cold tomato soup

helado ice cream
huevo egg
jamón serrano cured ham
judías beans
langosta lobster
leche milk
lomo pork loin
marisco shellfish
mejillones mussels
morcilla black pudding
pan bread
patatas fritas chips
pescado fish
picante spicy
pollo chicken
pulpo octopus
queso cheese
salchicha sausage
salsa sauce
ternera veal
tortilla omelette
trucha trout
verduras vegetables
vino wine

PLACES TO EAT

We have used the following symbols to give an idea of the price for an à la carte, three-course meal for one, with house wine:

€€€€	over 60 euros
€€€	40–60 euros
€€	25–40 euros
€	below 25 euros

CIUTAT VELLA (OLD TOWN)

Agut €€ *Carrer Gignàs 16, tel: 93-315 1709.* Tue–Sat lunch and dinner. This small restaurant, founded in 1924, is hidden away on a small street in the Barri Gòtic behind Passeig de Colom, not far from the main post office. Relaxed and homely, it has plenty of Catalan flavour and lots of daily specials, which might include home-made cannelloni, fish or game. The excellent and huge rice dishes are meant to be shared.

Biocenter € *Carrer del Pintor Fortuny 25, tel: 93-301 4583,* www.res taurantebiocenter.es. Mon–Thu 10am–11pm, Fri until 11.30pm, Sat 1pm–11.30pm, 1–4pm Sun. Vegetarian restaurant serving huge portions in a friendly atmosphere. Located just off La Rambla, north of the Mercat La Boqueria.

Cal Pep €€–€€€ *Plaça de les Olles 8, tel: 93-310 7961,* www.calpep.com. Mon dinner only, Tue–Sat lunch and dinner. A boisterous bar in a pretty square in El Born, just off Pla del Palau, this is the place for some of the best seafood in Barcelona – if you can get a seat. Reservations are only available for groups of four or more, and there's just one row of chairs at the counter and a few tables in the back room. The counter is the place to be. The display of baby squid, octopus, fried fish and mussels is amazing. Be prepared to queue, it's worth the wait.

Can Culleretes €–€€ *Carrer d'en Quintana 5, tel: 93-317 3022,* www.culle retes.com. Tue–Sat lunch and dinner, Sun lunch only. Barcelona's oldest restaurant has served traditional Catalan food since 1786. It is cosy and informal, and serves classics like *espinacs à la catalana* (spinach with pine nuts and raisins) and *botifarra* (spicy country sausage). Fixed-price menus available weekdays. Near La Rambla but feels like a different world.

Los Caracoles €€–€€€ *Carrer d'Escudellers 14, tel: 93-301 2041,* www.loscaracoles.es. Daily lunch and dinner. 'The Snails' is famous for its chicken roasting on a spit outside, on one of the Old Quarter's busiest pedestrian streets, just south of Plaça Reial. It has been around since 1835, and while it's touristy it is fun, and you can get a fine meal of fish, game, roasted chicken or lamb, in addition, of course, to snails.

La Dolça Herminia €€ *Carrer de les Magdalenes 27, tel: 93-317 0676,* www.grupandilana.com. Lunch and dinner daily. Close to Via Laietana, this smart but very reasonably priced establishment has an imaginative menu. No reservations.

Fonda España €€€ *Carrer de Sant Pau 9, tel: 93-550 0010,* www. hotelespanya.com. Mon–Sat lunch and dinner, Sun lunch only. A smart restaurant in the Hotel España, the gorgeous dining room was decorated by *modernista* architect Domènech i Montaner, while the back room has murals by Ramón Casas, a contemporary of Picasso. Renowned Michelin-starred chef, Martin Berasategui, brings new culinary delights at reasonable prices. Next to the Teatre del Liceu.

El Gran Café €€–€€€ *Carrer d'Avinyó 9, tel: 93-318 7986,* http://restaurantelgrancafe.com; Lunch and dinner daily Sun–Fri. Looks like an English pub on the outside, but has a handsome *modernista* interior, and is well-known for its Catalan cuisine. The set menu is very good value, otherwise it is rather expensive.

El Bosc de Les Fades €€ *Passatge de la Banca,7, tel: 93-317 2649.* Lunch and dinner daily. This restaurant – a surreal fairy tale escape from the world outside – is dramatically different from the other restaurants on this list or in this area. Tapas are served but it's the drinks and quirky surroundings that draw people in.

Els Quatre Gats (4 Gats) €€ *Carrer de Montsió 3, tel: 93-302 4140,* www.4gats.com. Daily 9am–midnight. 'The Four Cats', which was once the hangout of Picasso and friends, serves simple Catalan fare in fabulous *modernista* surroundings, with pictures of its illustrious clientele on the walls. The *menú del día* (lunch only) is a good deal, but really the atmosphere's the thing.

El Quim de la Boqueria €–€€ *Mercat La Boqueria, La Rambla, tel: 93-301 9810,* www.elquimdelaboqueria.com. Tue–Sat breakfast and lunch. This is one of several stalls in la Boqueria, on La Rambla, where it's a treat to pull up a stool and see the freshest produce grilled before your eyes. Don't be surprised to see locals eating a hearty breakfast of pigs' trotters washed down with a glass of red wine.

Rodrigo € *Carrer de l'Argenteria 67, tel: 93-310 3020.* Thu–Tue 9.30am–1am, Wed 6pm–1am. A real family-run local bar, not far from the church of Santa Maria del Mar, serving delicious set menus at a good price. Don't miss their pre-lunch *vermut*, an intoxicating house speciality.

Senyor Parellada €€–€€€ *Carrer de l'Argenteria 37, tel: 93-310 5094,* www.senyorparellada.com. Lunch and dinner daily. An attractive, popular restaurant in La Ribera, close to the church of Santa Maria del Mar. Both the surroundings and the creative Catalan menu are sophisticated but unpretentious.

Sesamo € *Carrer de Sant Antoni Abat 52, tel: 93-441 6411.* Daily 7pm–midnight. A bit off the beaten track, close to Sant Antoni market on the western edge of El Raval, this inviting vegetarian restaurant is worth a visit for its fantastic range of dishes and an excellent tapas tasting menu.

Shunka €€–€€€ *Carrer del Sagristans 5, tel: 93-412 4991,* www. koyshunka.com. Lunch and dinner Tue–Sun. Try sushi, sashimi and much more at this excellent Japanese restaurant hidden behind the cathedral. It's all cooked before your eyes.

TAPAS BARS

Bar Lobo €€ *Carrer del Pintor Fortuny, 3; tel: 93 481 53 46; www.grupotra galuz.com/restaurantes/bar-lobo.* Daily 9am–midnight. The hippest member of the Tragaluz empire attracts a cool crowd with its stylish interior, lounging terrace in a busy pedestrian street, and combination of light Mediterranean and Japanese dishes. Open late for drinks at weekends.

Bar Pinotxo €–€€ *Mercat La Boqueria, La Rambla, 89, tel: 93-317 1731.* Mon–Sat breakfast and lunch. This tiny, plain-looking bar with just a handful of stools is surrounded by La Boqueria's mesmerising produce. It's a terrific place to stop if you are shopping or sightseeing and your stomach's beginning to growl. The fish, as you would imagine, is incredibly fresh. Full lunch menu also available (recited orally, so it helps to know what some of the items are).

Euskal Etxea €€ *Placeta de Montcada 1–3, tel: 93-310 2185,* www.eu skaletxeataberna.com. Lunch and dinner daily. A great Basque tapas bar with a huge choice that has quickly established itself as a firm local favourite. Excellent meals served in the restaurant area, which are more expensive. Located at the bottom of Carrer de Montcada, south of the Museu Picasso.

Irati Taverna Basca €–€€ *Carrer del Cardenal Casañas 17, tel: 93-302 3084,* www.iratitavernabasca.com. Lunch and dinner daily. In the same group as Euskal Etxea, this immensely popular Basque tapas joint, just off La Rambla at the edge of the Barri Gòtic, is always packed. At lunchtime and in early evening, heaving trays of tapas (*pintxos* in Basque) are laid out on the bar. It's a bit like a party, except that you have to keep track of the number of tapas and the glasses of wine or beer you've had, and the cheerful attendants tally it all up before you leave. Full menu also available.

La Vinya del Senyor € *Plaça Santa Maria 5, tel: 93-310 3379.* Lunch and dinner daily. Delightful wine bar with a large terrace overlooking the facade of Santa Maria del Mar, in the Born. Offers interesting wines and *cava* by the glass, and a few select tapas to absorb the alcohol.

El Xampanyet € *Carrer de Montcada 22, tel: 93-319 7003*, www.elxampanyet.es. Tue–Sat lunch and dinner, Sun lunch only. Situated near the Museu Picasso and El Born, this *azulejo*-tiled bar specialises in cava and some of the best tapas in town, especially the Cantabrian anchovies. An old-school classic.

EIXAMPLE

La Bodegueta € *Rambla de Catalunya 100, tel: 93-215 4894, provenca.labodegueta.cat.* Mon–Sat breakfast, lunch and dinner, Sun lunch and dinner. It's easy to pass by this simple *bodega*, on the corner of La Rambla and Carrer de Provença, without even noticing it. Regulars pop in at any hour for *jamón serrano* (cured ham) and a glass of Rioja. Good wine selection. No credit cards.

Piscolabis €€ *Rambla de Catalunya 27, tel: 93-306 9669*, www.piscolabisrestaurant.es. Mon–Fri 8am–1am, Sat from 9am, Sun from 11am. Good value, and an excellent choice of tapas. The friendly service will make you feel right at home. Outside seating is available if you'd rather sit in the sun than the well-designed interior.

Casa Calvet €€€–€€€€ *Carrer de Casp 48, tel: 93-412 4012.* Mon–Sat lunch and dinner. Located on the ground floor of one of Antoni Gaudí's first apartment buildings, Casa Calvet exudes an elegant *modernista* ambience. The service is extraordinary, and the tables are spaced well apart. The Catalan menu is excellent and fairly priced. Nearest metro is Urquinaona.

Cinc Sentits €€€€ *Carrer d'Entença, 60, tel: 93-323 9490*, www.cincsentits.com. Tue–Sat lunch and dinner. An ideal choice for foodies: Michelin-starred chef Jordi Artal's tasting menu is a guaranteed gourmet experience and a good example of new Catalan cuisine. It's at the intersection of the streets d'Aribau and d'Aragó.

Roast Club Café €€ *Carrer de València, 143; tel: 65- 788 1466*, https://roastclubcafe.com. Tue–Sun breakfast, lunch, and dinner. Some of the finest coffee in the city can be found here. They also serve delicious sandwiches, salads, and cakes.

Madrid-Barcelona €€ *Carrer d'Aragó 282, tel: 93-853 3085.* Lunch and dinner daily. Located just off Passeig de Gràcia, this pleasantly old-fashioned place has a good selection of Catalan and regional Spanish dishes.

Moments €€€€ *Hotel Mandarin Oriental, Passeig de Gràcia 38–40, tel: 93-151 8781, www.mandarinoriental.com.* Tue–Sat lunch and dinner. With a Michelin star, Moments is certainly impressive and proving a popular chic, fine-dining venue. Overseen by the only female chef to hold seven Michelin stars, Carme Ruscalleda, the menu sees a return to traditional Catalan roots.

Taktika Berri €€–€€€ *Carrer de València 169, tel: 93-453 4759.* Mon–Fri lunch and dinner, Sat lunch only. Basque cooking is the finest regional cuisine in Spain, and Basque restaurants are popping up everywhere. One of the best in Barcelona is this family-owned and operated tapas bar and restaurant in a converted textile workshop, close to the intersection of streets València and Muntaner. The *pintxos* (tapas) are excellent, as are their creative entrées and splendid desserts.

Tapas 24 €–€€ *Carrer de la Diputació 269, tel: 93-488 0977; www.carlesabellan.com.* Daily 9am–midnight. At this trendy bar, not far from Girona metro, you can taste classic tapas by maestro Carles Abellan, one of a new generation of Catalan star chefs. You might have to queue, but it's worth it and the bustling atmosphere is absorbing.

Tragaluz €€€–€€€€ *Passatge de la Concepció 5, tel: 93-487 0621, www.grupotragaluz.com.* Lunch and dinner daily. Barcelona's love affair with food comes to life in this trendy, colourful restaurant on a tiny passageway off Passeig de Gràcia. After a complete overhaul, Tragaluz (Skylight), allows you to dine under a glass roof, and has a new, fresh approach. The Mediterranean cuisine still hits the mark but with a lighter touch. Alternatively you can dine on oysters, sushi or Japanese grilled food at the bars downstairs.

WATERFRONT/PORT OLÍMPIC

Agua €€–€€€ *Passeig Marítim 30, tel: 93-225 1272, www.grupotragaluz.com.* Daily 9am–11.30pm, Fri–Sat until 12.30am. Almost on the beach, with indoor and outdoor tables, the modern and attractive Agua gets very busy, so booking is essential, especially if you want to sit on the terrace. Well-prepared fish, rice dishes such as risottos, and imaginative vegetarian dishes.

Can Ganassa €–€€ *Plaça de la Barceloneta 6, tel: 93-252 8449*, www. restaurantcanganassa.es. Lunch and dinner daily. A popular seafood restaurant on the main square in Barceloneta serving excellent fish dishes as well as a wide array of delicious tapas and sandwiches.

Can Majó €€–€€€ *Carrer de l'Almirante Aixada 23, tel: 93-221 5455*, www. canmajo.es. Tue–Sat lunch and dinner, Sun lunch only. It's difficult to find a really authentic paella, but at this Barceloneta classic you can't go wrong. Pleasant dining rooms and a terrace facing the sea.

Xiroi Ca la Nuri €€–€€€ *Passeig Marítim de la Nova Icària, 38, tel: 93-221 3558*, www.xiroi.calanuri.com. Lunch and dinner daily. A dependable seafood restaurant known for its rice dishes, tapas, and fish dishes. This location has been serving the local Catalan community since 1950.

Restaurant 7 Portes €€€ *Passeig d'Isabel II 14, tel: 93-319 3033*, www.7portes.com. Lunch and dinner daily. Not far from the *Cap de Barcelona* artwork, this is one of Barcelona's most venerable institutions, now sympathetically restored, and a favourite for business meals and special occasions since 1836. Restaurant 7 Portes (meaning seven doors) is famous for its rice dishes; favourites include black rice with squid in its own ink and an assortment of paellas. Portions are very large, the dining rooms are elegant and the waiters are old-style attentive.

Xiringuíto Escribà €€–€€€ *Avinguda Litoral Mar 62, Platja Bogatell, tel: 93-221 0729*; http://xiringuitoescriba.com. Daily lunch and dinner. Lots of imaginative fish and rice dishes in this down-to-earth, family-run establishment, right by the beach, east of Port Olímpic. And, yes, they are the same Escribà family that is renowned for their chocolates and pastries, so the puddings are guaranteed to be marvellous.

GRÀCIA AND ABOVE THE DIAGONAL

Bilbao €€–€€€ *Carrer del Perill 33, tel: 93-458 9624;* www.restau rantbilbao.com. Mon–Sat lunch and dinner. Best at lunch time when the local crowd are there, this bustling restaurant has heaps of atmosphere and uses the freshest market produce. It's across the Avinguda Diagonal northwest of Diagonal metro, off Carrer de Corsega.

Botafumeiro €€€€ *Carrer Gran de Gràcia 81, tel: 93-218 4230,* www. botafumeiro.es. Lunch and dinner daily. This is Barcelona's top seafood restaurant and it is said to be the King of Spain's favourite. It's large and informal, with lots of action. Much of the fresh seafood is flown in daily from the owner's home territory, Galicia. You can get great shellfish and seafood tapas here (which keeps costs down). To get a seat at the seafood bar, visit off-hours, earlier than local people would eat – as the restaurant opens at 1pm for lunch, and 7–8pm for dinner. Just above the Diagonal, at the beginning of the Gràcia neighbourhood.

A–Z TRAVEL TIPS

A SUMMARY OF PRACTICAL INFORMATION

A

ACCOMMODATION (see also the list of Recommended Hotels starting on page 133)

Following fevered construction over the last decade, as well as renovation of old buildings and palaces, there are about 70.000 hotel beds in the city with still more on the way. This supply makes it possible to get some good deals off-season, especially if booked online in advance. It can still be difficult to find a central hotel when a trade fair is taking place or over main holiday periods, though there are plenty of other options. Tourist apartments are the new favourite, many old buildings having been converted into apartments for this sole purpose. A few guesthouses *(hostals, pensions)* and even youth hostels *(albergs juvenils)* are becoming 'boutique', and B&Bs are on the rise. Hotels can be booked via the tourist office (tel: 933 689 700 www.barcelonaturisme.com).

For apartment rental, try the following agencies: Apartments Inside Barcelona (www.inside-bcn.com); Oh-Barcelona (www.oh-barcelona.com); Destination BCN (www.destinationbcn.com); Apartment Barcelona (www.apartmentbarcelona.com). For B&Bs try BCN Home (www.bcn-home.com).

I'd like a double/single room. **Quisiera una habitación doble/sencilla.**
with/without bath/shower **con/sin baño/ducha**
double bed **cama matrimonial**
What's the rate per night? **¿Cuál es el precio por noche?**
Is breakfast included? **¿Está incluído el desayuno?**

AIRPORTS

Barcelona's international airport, El Prat de Llobregat (tel: 902-404 704, www.aena.es) is 12km (7 miles) south of the city. You can get into Barcelona by train, bus, metro, taxi or rent a car. The national train service, RENFE (tel: 912-320 320, www.renfe.com), runs trains from the airport every half hour, stopping at Barcelona Sants and Passeig de Gràcia, taking about 30 minutes. The fare is about €4.20, though it is worth buying a T10 card (see page 131). The recently renovated metro line L9 stops at both terminals and connects with three urban metro lines (L1, L3, L5). Note that a special ticket €4.50 is needed to ride the airport line. Two different Aerobuses (tel: 93-415 6020, www.aerobusbcn.com) depart every 5–10 minutes from each terminal for Pl. Catalunya, daily 5.35am–1.00am, stopping at several points en route. The fare is €5.90 single, €10.20 return. There is also a public bus (no.46) linking the airport terminals with Pl. Espanya in the city centre. Taxis charge about €30 to the city centre. Agree a fare before you start. They can charge extra for luggage.

B

BICYCLE RENTAL

Cycles can be rented at several outlets, such as Budget Bikes on Calle Estruc 38 (tel: 93-304 1885, www.budgetbikes.eu), or Green Bikes on Carrer Escudellers 48 (tel: 93 301 36 12; www.greenbikesbarcelona. com); both offer tours.

BUDGETING FOR YOUR TRIP

Barcelona has become much more expensive than it used to be and is on a par with other major European cities in many respects.

Transport to Barcelona. By budget airline or via Girona or Reus, getting to Barcelona can be the cheapest part of your trip, from as little as €30 off-season, but obviously much more (€150–300 or more) on scheduled flights or from outside Europe. Buy in advance for the best deals.

Accommodation. Most hotels do not include breakfast or the 10 percent VAT in their prices. Youth hostel €15–45 per person in a dorm; €40–80 in a *pension*; €90–225 en suite double room; €225–450 top end. Note that these prices are average ranges, some specifics places may be much more expensive.

Meals. Restaurants are no longer cheap, but good deals can be found. The *menú del día*, a fixed-price midday meal, is excellent value from €12 upward. Spanish wines are usually reasonably priced, even in fine restaurants. A three-course evening meal in a mid-range restaurant with house wine: €30–50 per person.

Drinks. Mineral water €0.80–3; coffee €1.50–4; fresh orange juice €3–4; *caña* (small draught beer) €2–4; glass of wine €3–4; spirit with mixer €4–7 or higher in clubs.

Local transport. Public transport within the city – buses and the metro – is inexpensive (see page 130) and taxis are reasonably priced.

Attractions. Museums and attractions range from free to over €17. Most municipal museums are free from 3pm on Sundays. The Art Ticket (www.articketbcn.org) is good value at €30, as it allows entrance to six art centres. Purchase online, at one of the centres or at tourist offices.

C

CAR HIRE

Unless you plan to travel a good deal throughout Catalonia, there is no need to hire a car. Barcelona has considerable parking problems and general congestion, and a car is more trouble than it's worth.

If you do wish to hire a car, however, major international and Spanish companies have offices in the airport and in the city centre. A value-added tax (IVA) of 21 percent is added to the total charge, but will have been in-

I'd like to rent a car **Quisiera alquilar un coche**
for tomorrow **para mañana**
for one day/a week **por un día/una semana**
Please include full risk insurance. **Haga el favor de incluir el seguro a todo riesgo.**
Fill it up, please. **Lleno, por favor.**
May I return it to the airport? **¿Puedo dejarlo al aeropuerto?**

cluded if you have pre-paid before arrival (lowest rates are normally found online). Shorter rentals usually cost more per day than longer ones; three days' rental for a medium-sized family car costs €85–250 (more in peak season). Fully comprehensive insurance is required and should be included in the price; confirm that this is the case. Most companies require you to pay by credit card, or use your card as a deposit/guarantee. You must be over 21 and have had a licence for at least 6 months. A national driver's licence will suffice for EU nationals; others need an international licence.

CLIMATE

Barcelona's mild Mediterranean climate assures sunshine most of the year and makes freezing temperatures rare even in the depths of winter (December to February). Spring and autumn are the most agreeable seasons for visiting. Midsummer can be hot and humid; at times a thick smog hangs over the city. Average temperatures are given below.

	J	F	M	A	M	J	J	A	S	O	N	D
°F	49	51	54	59	64	72	75	75	71	63	56	51
°C	9	10	12	14	18	22	24	24	22	18	13	11

CLOTHING

Barceloneses are very stylish and fashion-conscious. Smart-casual clothing is what visitors generally need. Men are expected to wear a jacket in better restaurants. You won't see many local people eating out in shorts and trainers, except in beachside cafés. From November to April you'll need a warm jacket or jumper and raincoat. The rest of the year, light summer clothing is in order.

CRIME AND SAFETY

You should exercise caution and be on your guard against pickpockets and bag snatchers (be wary of people offering 'assistance'), especially on or near La Rambla, the old city (particularly El Raval) and other major tourist areas, such as La Sagrada Família and crowded spots such as markets. Take the same precautions as you would at home. Photocopy personal documents and leave the originals in your hotel.

The blue-clad, mobile anti-crime squads are out in force on the Ramblas and principal thoroughfares. Should you be the victim of a crime, make a *denuncia* (report) at the nearest police station (*comisaría* – vital if you are going to make an insurance claim). The main one in the Old Town is at Nou de la Rambla 76–78, or call the Mossos d'Esquadra on 091 or 112. You can also report theft at most city hotels.

> I want to report a theft. **Quiero denunciar un robo.**
> My handbag/wallet/passport has been stolen. **Me han robado el bolso/la cartera/el pasaporte.**
> Help! Thief! **¡Socorro! ¡Ladrón!**

D

DISABLED TRAVELLERS

Barcelona has plenty of hotels with facilities (see www.barcelona-access.cat, or check with the tourist office). Many museums and historic buildings are wheelchair-accessible. The beaches have suitable access, and there are many adapted public toilets. Some bus and metro lines have facilities for disabled travellers (see www.tmb.cat). For adapted taxi information, contact 93-420 8088.

DRIVING

In the event of a problem, drivers need a passport, a valid driving licence, registration papers and Green Card international insurance.
Road Conditions. Roads within Barcelona are very congested and the ring roads around the city can be confusing. Roads and highways out-

side Barcelona are excellent, though you'll have to pay a toll *(peaje/peatje)* on most motorways *(autopistas)*. To cross into France via the La Jonquera border (160km/100 miles) from Barcelona, take the AP7 or E15 motorway. For road information, tel: 900-123 505.

Rules and Regulations. Your car should display a nationality sticker. Front and rear seatbelts, a spare set of bulbs, visibility vests and two warning triangles are compulsory. Most fines for traffic offences are payable on the spot. Drive on the right, overtake on the left and give right of way to vehicles coming from the right (unless your road is marked as having priority). Speed limits are 120kmh (75mph) on motorways, 100kmh (62mph) on dual carriageways, 90kmh (56mph) on main roads, 50kmh (30mph), or as marked, in urban areas. Speed checks are regular. The roads are patrolled by the Mossos d'Esquadra. The permitted blood-alcohol level is low and penalties stiff.

Registration papers **Permiso de circulación**
Is this the right road for...? **Es ésta la carretera hacia...?**
Full tank, please. **Lléne el depósito, por favor.**
normal/super **normal/super**
Please check the oil/tyres/battery. **Por favor, controle el aceite/los neumáticos/la batería.**
Can I park here? **¿Se puede aparcar aquí?**
My car has broken down. **Mi coche se ha estropeado.**
There's been an accident. **Ha habido un accidente.**
(International) driving licence **Carnet de conducir (internacional)**
Car registration papers **Permiso de circulación**
Green card **Tarjeta verde**

Road signs. You may see the following written signs in Spanish:
Parking. Finding a place to park can be difficult in Barcelona. Look for

'blue zones' (denoted by a blue 'P'), which are metered areas, or underground parking garages (also marked with a big blue-and-white 'P'). Green zones are reserved for residents with permits.

Breakdowns and Assistance. In emergencies, tel: **112.**

> **¡Alto!** Stop!
> **Aparcamiento** Parking
> **Autopista** Motorway
> **Ceda el paso** Give way (yield)
> **Cruce peligroso** Dangerous crossroads
> **Curva peligrosa** Dangerous bend
> **Despacio** Slow
> **Peligro** Danger
> **Prohibido adelantar** No overtaking (passing)
> **Prohibido aparcar** No parking

E

ELECTRICITY

The standard is 220 volts. Power sockets (outlets) take round, two-pin plugs, so you will need an international adapter plug.

> an adapter/a battery **un transformador/una pila/una batería**

EMBASSIES AND CONSULATES

All embassies are in Madrid, but most Western European countries have consulates in Barcelona. A few notable Consulates are listed below:

Canada: Pl. de Catalunya 9, 1º, 2a, tel: 93-412 7236.

Ireland: Gran Vía Carlos III 94, tel: 93-491 5021.

New Zealand: Travessera de Gràcia 64, 2º, tel: 93-209 0399.
South Africa: Parc Empresarial Mas Blau II, c/ Alta Ribagorça, 6–8, Prat de Llobregat, tel: 93-506 9100.
UK: Avda Diagonal 477, 13º, tel: 93-366 6200, www.gov.uk.
US: Passeig de la Reina Elisenda 23, tel: 93-280 2227, https://es.usembassy.gov.

EMERGENCIES (see also Police, and Crime and Safety)

General emergencies: **112**
Mossos d'Esquadra (Autonomous Catalan Police): **091**
Municipal (city) police: **092**
Fire: **080**
Ambulance: **061**

Police! **¡Policía!**
Fire! **¡Fuego!**
Stop! **¡Para!/¡Deténagase!**
Help! **¡Socorro!**
Thief! **¡Ladrón!**

G

GETTING THERE

By Air (see also Airports). Barcelona's airport is linked by regularly scheduled, daily non-stop flights from across Europe. Some flights from the US and Canada are direct; others go through Madrid (or in some cases, Lisbon). From Australia, Singapore and New Zealand, regular one-stop flights go directly to Barcelona or Madrid. Flying times: London, about 2 hours; New York, approximately 8 hours.

Iberia, the Spanish national airline, covers most countries in shared arrangements with their own carriers. Contact Iberia in the UK: tel: 036

843 774, www.iberia.com.

As well as regularly scheduled flights there is a good choice of discounts and charter flights from companies such as EasyJet (www.easyjet.com). As well as flying to El Prat, Ryanair (www.ryanair.com) flies to Barcelona El Prat, **Girona** (90km/56 miles from Barcelona) or **Reus** (80km/50 miles from Barcelona) from several UK cities. Girona and Reus airports have shuttle bus connections to Barcelona (check timetables – Girona: www.sagales.com; Reus: www.igualadina.com). **Lleida-Alguaire** airport in Western Catalonia, which opened in 2010, receives some charter flights from the UK. Spanish airline Vueling (www.vueling.com) is a budget airline.

By Sea. Balearia has a service to/from Ibiza, Mallorca and Menorca (tel: 902 160 180; www.balearia.com). Acciona-Trasmediterránea (Moll Sant Bertran 3; tel: 902-454 645; www.trasmediterranea.es) also operates ferries to the Balearic Islands. Grimaldi Lines (www.grimaldi-lines.com) go to/from Civitavecchia (70km from Rome).

By Rail. The Spanish rail network has been greatly modernised in recent years. Nowadays you can catch high-speed, sleeper services to Barcelona from several European destinations. Renfe-SNCF (www.renfe-sncf.com) and others arrive in Barcelona from cities such as Paris, Milan, and Zurich. Once completed, the La Sagrera station can expect more high-speed rail links to other parts of Europe. Trains run four times a day between Barcelona Sants station and Montpellier (www.raileurope.co.uk), where you can connect with the TGV, the French high-speed train. The AVE, the Spanish high-speed train, runs several times a day between Barcelona and Madrid.

RENFE is the Spanish national rail network (tel: 912-320 320, www.renfe.com). Local trains in Catalonia, Ferrocarrils Generalitat de Catalunya (FGC; www.fgc.cat), are serviced by the Catalan government.

RENFE honours InterRail, Rail Plus and Eurail cards (the latter sold only outside Europe), and offers substantial discounts to people under 26, senior citizens (over 60) as well as large families. It is well worthwhile finding out about current discount tickets from a travel agency, station, or, in Barcelona, from the information desk in Sants station or by phoning RENFE on the number given above.

By Car. The highways outside Barcelona are generally excellent. The AP7 motorway leads to Barcelona from France and northern Catalonia; the AP2 leads to Barcelona from Madrid, Zaragoza and Bilbao. From Valencia or the Costa del Sol, take the E15 north.

By Bus. Several bus companies operate a service to Barcelona, the largest of which is Eurolines (tel: 932 650 788, www.eurolines.es). Most arrive at the bus station Barcelona Nord (tel: 902-260 606), but some go to Barcelona Sants. For more information and schedules, see www. barcelonanord.com.

GUIDES AND TOURS

English-speaking, licensed guides and interpreters may be arranged through the Barcelona Guide Bureau (tel: 93-268 2422; www.barcelo naguidebureau.com).

Tours by bus: Barcelona Bus Turístic (www.barcelonabusturistic.cat) offers a tour with three different routes; hop on and off as you please. Two depart from Plaça de Catalunya, one from Port Olímpic from 9am daily; all stops have full timetables. Complete journey time is about 2 hours, or 40 minutes for the Port Olímpic route. Tickets may be purchased online, at Turisme de Barcelona Tourist Information Points, at newspaper kiosks, bookshops and hotels.

On foot: Barcelona Free Walking Tours runs English-speaking, guided tours of the Gothic quarter daily at 11am and 3pm. Walks (lasting approx. 2 hours) begin at Turisme de Barcelona (Plaça de Catalunya, tel: 622 940 471). Walks should be booked in advance at a tourist office. Other themed tours are available (Craft Tours, Bike Tours).

H

HEALTH AND MEDICAL CARE

Visitors from EU countries with corresponding health insurance facilities are entitled to medical and hospital treatment under the Spanish social security system – you need a European Health Insurance Card

(EHIC), obtainable from post offices or online. However, it does not cover everything and it is advisable to take out private medical insurance, which should be part of a travel insurance package. The water is safe to drink, but bottled water is always safest.

In an emergency, go to a main hospital: Hospital Clinic on Villarroel 170 (tel: 93 227 54 00; www.hospitalclinic.org); Hospital Dos de Maig on Carrer del Dos de Maig 301 (tel: 93-507 27 00; www.csi.cat). For an ambulance, make your way to an *ambulatorio* (medical centre) or tel: **061**.

Pharmacies *(farmacias)* are open during normal business hours but there is generally one in each district that remains open all night and on holidays. The location and phone number of this *farmacia de guardia* is posted on the door of all the others, and carried in daily newspapers. Tel: **098** for this information.

> Where's the nearest (all-night) pharmacy? **¿Donde está la farmacia (de guardia) más cercana?**
> I need a doctor/dentist. **Necesito un médico/dentista.**

L

LGBTQ TRAVELLERS

Barcelona has an active gay community and scores of clubs and nightlife options. The gay and lesbian hotline is 900-601 601. The website www.barcelona.com/barcelona_city_guide/gay contains information and listings.

LANGUAGE

Both Catalan *(catalá)* and Castilian Spanish *(castellano)* are official languages in Catalonia; everyone in Barcelona who speaks Catalan can speak Castilian Spanish but many will not unless absolutely necessary. Street signs are in Catalan. Spanish (Castilian) will get you by, so most of the language tips in this section are given in Spanish.

English – *Catalan* – **Castilian**
Good morning – *Bon dia* – **Buenos días**
Good afternoon – *Bona tarda* – **Buenas tardes**
Goodnight – *Bona nit* – **Buenas noches**
Goodbye – *Adéu* – **Adiós**
Hello – *Hola* – **Hola**
See you later – *Fins desprès* – **Hasta luego**
Please – *Si us plau* – **Por favor**
Thank you – *Gràcies* – **Gracias**
You're welcome – *De res* – **De nada**
Welcome – *Benvinguts* – **Bienvenido**
Do you speak English? –*¿Parla anglés?* – **¿Habla inglés?**
I don't understand. – *No ho entenc* – **No entiendo**
How much is it? –*¿Quant es?* – **¿Cuánto vale?**
Open/closed – *obert/tancat* – **abierto/cerrado**

M

MAPS

The Guía Urbana de *Barcelona* handbook is the most comprehensive and useful street map, but more manageable maps are available at the tourist office or on newsstands on La Rambla.

I'd like a street plan/a road map of this region **Quisiera un plano de la ciudad/un mapa de carreteras de esta región**

MEDIA

Most European newspapers and the Paris-based *International Herald Tribune* are sold on the day of publication at newsstands in the Ramblas and Passeig de Gràcia and in FNAC in Plaça de Catalunya. *Metropolitan* (www.barcelona-metropolitan.com), Barcelona's first monthly magazine in English, is free and has useful listings. For Spanish speakers the *Guía del Ocio (Leisure Guide)* lists bars and restaurants, along with cinema, theatre and concert performances.

MONEY

Currency *(moneda)*. The monetary unit of Spain is the euro (symbolised €). Notes are issued in denominations of 5, 10, 20, 50, 100, 200 and 500 euros. Coins in circulation are 1, 2, 5, 10, 20 and 50 cents, and 1 and 2 euros.

Currency exchange *(cambio)*. Banks and *cajas/caixes* (savings banks) are the best place to exchange currency, offering the best rates with no commission. Many travel agencies and currency exchange offices (displaying a *cambio* sign) also exchange foreign currency, and stay open outside banking hours. Banks and exchange offices pay slightly more for travellers' cheques than for cash. Always take your passport when you go to change money. Otherwise, there are several currency exchange spots spread around the city. Rates can fluctuate heavily so pay special attention.

Credit cards *(tarjetas de crédito)*. Photo identification is usually requested when paying with a card; some businesses may insist on looking at your passport.

Travellers' cheques *(cheques de viajero)*. Hotels, shops, restaurants

Where's the nearest bank/currency exchange office?
¿Dónde está el banco/la casa de cambio más cercana?
I want to change some pounds/dollars **Quiero cambiar libras/dólares**
Do you accept travellers' cheques? **¿Aceptan cheques de viajero?**
Can I pay with a credit card? **¿Se puede pagar con tarjeta?**
How much is that? **¿Cuánto es/Cuánto vale?**

and travel agencies may cash travellers' cheques, and so do some banks, where the process is more complicated, but you are likely to get a better rate. You will always need your passport.

O

OPENING TIMES

Shops. The bigger stores and shopping malls open 10am–9 or 10pm, but smaller shops close in the early afternoon (for lunch). Usual hours are Mon–Sat 9am–1.30pm and 4.30–8pm or later, although these do vary.

Banks. Generally open Mon–Fri 8.30am–2pm; in winter also Sat 8.30am–1pm.

Government offices and most businesses. Open Mon–Fri 8/9am–2pm and 4–6/7pm. In summer, many businesses work *horas intensivas*, from 8am–3pm, to avoid the hottest part of the day.

Museums. Most Tue–Sat 10am–8pm and Sun 10am–2.30pm. Some close for lunch. Most close on Mondays, with exceptions. Some have later hours in summer on Thursday and Friday, often with bar service.

P

POLICE

In Barcelona, dial **092** for municipal (city) police and **112** for the autonomous Catalan police. The main police station in the Old Town is at Nou de la Rambla 76–78.

Where's the nearest police station? **¿Dónde está la comisaría más cercana?**

POST OFFICES

Post offices are identified by yellow-and-white signs with a crown and the words 'Correos y Telégrafos'. The postal system is pretty reliable. Opening hours are usually Mon–Fri 8.30am–8.30pm and Sat 9am–1pm. The central post office, in Plaça d'Antonio López (tel: 93-486 8302), at the port end of Via Laietana, is open Mon–Fri 8.30am–9.30pm and Sat 8.30am–2pm.

Stamps (sellos) can be purchased at the post office or more easily at estancos/estancs (tobacconists) – look for the brown-and-yellow sign that reads 'Tabacs'. Allow about one week for delivery to North America, and 4–5 days to the UK. To speed things up, send a letter urgente (express) or certificado (registered). Postboxes are yellow.

Where is the post office? **¿Dónde está el correo?**
A stamp for this letter/ postcard, please. **Por favor, un sello para esta carta/tarjeta postal**
I'd like to send this letter. **Me gustaría enviar esta carta.**
airmail **vía aérea**
express (special delivery) **urgente**
registered **certificado**
How long will it take to arrive? **¿Cuánto tarda en llegar?**

PUBLIC HOLIDAYS

1 January Año Nuevo, New Year's Day
6 January Epifanía/Los Reyes, Epiphany
1 May Fiesta de Trabajo, Labour Day
23/24 June Sant Joan, St Joan's Day
15 August Asunción, Assumption
11 September La Diada, Catalan National Day
24 September La Mercè (Mercedes), Barcelona's patron saint
1 November Todos los Santos, All Saints' Day
6 December Día de la Constitución, Constitution Day
8 December Inmaculada Concepción, Immaculate Conception
25–26 December Navidad, Christmas

Movable dates:
Feb/March *Mardi Gras*, Shrove Tuesday (Carnival)
Late March/April *Viernes Santo*, Good Friday
Late March/April *Lunes de Pascua*, Easter Monday
Mid-June *Corpus Christi*, Corpus Christi

T

TELEPHONES

Spain's country code is **34**. Barcelona's local area code, **93**, must be dialled before all phone numbers, even for local calls and from abroad (00 34 93 etc.).

As with most places public phones have gone the way of the dodo in Barcelona due to the ubiquity of mobile phones.

To make an international call, dial 00 for an international line + the country code + phone number, omitting any initial zero. Calls are cheaper after 10pm on weekdays, after 2pm on Saturday, and all day Sunday. Dial **1009** for operator assistance within Spain, 1008 for assistance within Europe and North Africa and **1005** for the rest of the world.

You can also make calls at public telephone offices called *locutorios*. A clerk will place the call for you and you pay for it afterwards. These tend to double as internet centres too. There are a few of them spread out throughout the city and can often be recognized by the internet services they also offer.

It can be very costly using your mobile in Spain and texting is by far the cheapest way of keeping in touch. Frequent callers might consider buying a SIM card for Spain on arrival. The main providers in Spain are Vodafone, Orange, Movistar and Yoigo. To phone the UK from your mobile dial 00 (+) 44 and the number, omitting the first 0.

TIME ZONES

Spanish time is the same as that in most of Western Europe – Greenwich Mean Time plus one hour. Clocks go forward one hour in spring and back one hour in autumn, so Spain is generally one hour ahead of London.

TIPPING

Since a service charge is normally included on hotel and restaurant bills, tipping is not obligatory but it's usual to leave small change (about 5 percent of the bill) on a bar counter, and 5–10 percent on restaurant bills. If you tip taxi drivers, 5 percent is enough. Additional guidelines: hotel porter, per bag: €1–2; lavatory attendant: 50 cents; tour guide: 10 percent; hairdresser: 10 percent; maid: €1–3 per day.

TOILETS

Toilet doors are distinguished in Catalan by an 'H' for *Homes* (men) or 'D' for *Dones* (women).

Where are the toilets? **¿Dónde están los servicios?**

TOURIST INFORMATION

Tourist Offices Abroad

Canada: 2 Bloor St West, Suite 3402, Toronto, Ontario M4W 3E2, tel: 416-961 3131.

Ireland: Callaghan House, 13-16 Dame Street, D02 HX67 Dublín, tel.:+353 016350200

UK: Spanish Tourist Office, 6th Floor, 64 North Row, London W1K 7DE, tel: 020-7317 2011. This office is open to the public by appointment only. Catalan Tourist Office: 17 Fleet Street (3rd Floor), London EC4Y 1AA, tel: 020-7583 8855.

US: Water Tower Place, Suite 915 East, 845 North Michigan Avenue, Chicago, IL 60611, tel: 312-642 1992.

8383 Wilshire Boulevard, Suite 960, 90211 Beverly Hills, CA 90211, tel: 323-658 7195.

60 East 42nd Street, 53rd floor, New York, NY 10165, tel: 212-265 8822. 2655 Le Jeune Rd (Gables International Plaza), Suite 605. Coral Gables, Miami, FL 33134; tel: 305 774 9643.

Barcelona Tourist Offices. The main tourist office is Turisme de Barcelona, Plaça de Catalunya 17, below street level (tel: 93-368 9700; www.barcelonaturisme.com), open daily 8.30am–9.00pm. The tourist information office in the Ajuntament (Town Hall), Plaça Sant Jaume, is open Mon–Fri 8.30am–8.30pm, Sat 9am–7pm, Sun 9am–2pm. Informació Turística de Catalunya in Palau Robert, Passeig de Gràcia 107 (tel: 93-292 1260 ; www.gencat.cat), provides information about Catalonia. There are also offices at Sants Station, the airport and on Plaça del Portal de la Pau.

TRANSPORT

Getting around town is easy, rapid and inexpensive. Transport information: www.tmb.cat or www.renfe.com.

By Metro. The metro (tel: 902 075 027; www.tmb.cat) is the fastest and easiest way to navigate the city. Stations are marked by a red diamond symbol. The metro runs Mon–Thur, Sun and holidays 5am–midnight, Fri 5am–2am; Sat 24 hours. Maps are available at metro stations, or consult the metro map at the back of this guide.

By Bus *(autobús)*. Barcelona buses (tel: 902 075 027; www.tmb.cat) have routes and hours clearly marked at the stops. You may have trouble recognising where you are, and most bus drivers speak no English, but buses are a good way of getting to see more of the city. They run daily 4.25am–11pm (variable depending on route), and there are infrequent night buses from 10.40pm to 5am.

The official Tourist Bus, which passes numerous interesting sights in the city is excellent; you can jump on and off at any stop (see page 122). An air-conditioned bus, rather unfortunately called the 'Tomb Bus', runs during business hours from the Plaça de Catalunya to the uptown Plaça Pius XII, covering all the smart shopping areas.

By Train. FGC (Ferrocarrils Generalitat de Catalunya; tel: 900 901 515;

www.fgc.cat) trains are useful for reaching Barcelona's upper neighbourhoods Sarrià, Pedralbes and Tibidabo, the Parc de Collserola
behind Tibidabo and nearby towns such as Sant Cugat, Terrassa and
Sabadell. These run from Plaça de Catalunya. The FGC trains also run
from Plaça Espanya to Montserrat, Colònia Güell and other destinations.

Tickets. You can buy a single ticket from the driver on buses, or a multiple card *(tarjeta multi-viaje T10)*, which is punched once you are inside the bus or in an automatic machine as you enter the station. This
is valid for bus, metro and urban FGC lines and allows transfer from
one means of transport to the other with no extra charge, within a time
limit. It works out at nearly half the price of the equivalent in single
tickets. Buy the T10 at stations, banks or *estancs*. The T10 can also be
used on RENFE trains within Zone 1, which includes the airport (but it's
not valid on the metro line connecting the airport with the city).

When's the next bus/train to...? **¿Cuándo sale el próximo
    autobús/tren para...?**
bus station **estación de autobuses**
A ticket to... **Un billete para...**
single (one-way) **ida**
return (round-trip) **ida y vuelta**
How much is the fare to...? **¿Cuánto es la tarifa a ...?**

By Taxi. Black-and-yellow taxis are everywhere and not too expensive.
During the day, they aren't your best option, as traffic is very heavy in
the city. At night, especially if you're in the old quarter, taxis are a good
option although they have a surcharge. Hail a cab in the street or pick
one up where they're lined up. A green light and/or a *libre* (vacant) sign
shows when the cab is empty.

Reputable taxi companies include Taxi Amic (tel: 93-420 8088), Radi-
otaxi 033 (tel: 93-303 3033) and the online company www.taxivallesbcn.

es. Check the fare before you get in; rates are fixed and are displayed in several languages on the window.

V

VISAS AND ENTRY REQUIREMENTS

Members of EU countries need only a passport. Visas are needed by non-EU nationals unless their country has a reciprocal agreement with Spain.

W

WEBSITES AND INTERNET ACCESS

The following websites provide plenty of useful information:
Barcelona Ajuntament (City Hall): www.barcelona.cat
Barcelona Tourist Information: www.barcelonaturisme.com
Catalonia on the web: http://web.gencat.cat/
Spain on the web: www.spain.info
National Tourist Office: www.tourspain.es

There are numerous internet cafés and access points in Barcelona, but be aware they are notorious for going out of business. Most cafés and hotels have Wi-Fi.

Y

YOUTH HOSTELS

The following youth hostels get very busy in the summer months, so it is advisable to book in advance: Alberg Juvenil Palau, Carrer Palau 6, tel: 93-412 5080; Equity Point Gothic, Carrer Vigatans 5, tel: 93-231 2045, www.equity-point.com; Kabul, Plaça Reial 17, tel: 93-3318 5190, www.kabul.es; Mare de Déu de Montserrat, Mare de Déu de Coll 41–52, tel: 93-210 5151; Pere Tarrès, Numància 149, tel: 93-410 2309, www.peretarres.org/alberg

RECOMMENDED HOTELS

Hotels of greatest interest to most visitors are those in the Eixample, the commercial and modernista grid north of Plaça de Catalunya, or in the Ciutat Vella (Old Town), which includes La Rambla, Barri Gòtic and the Born. The Old Town provides the best choice of pensions and inexpensive hotels, though visitors who stay on or near La Rambla have to tolerate late-night noise and crowds. Likewise, traffic noise can be a problem at many Eixample hotels.

Further away from the centre, better deals are available and these are a good option when you consider that the city's efficient public transport system can whisk you to the centre in a matter of minutes. The most recent additions are along the Waterfront and Diagonal Mar, where high-standard accommodation can be found at a reasonable price. The advantages of sea views and more peaceful nights, not to mention speedy access to the beach, make these areas well worth considering.

The following guide indicates prices for a double room in high season (prices should be used as an approximate guide only):

€€€€	over 200 euros
€€€	140–200 euros
€€	70–140 euros
€	below 70 euros

CIUTAT VELLA

Barceló Raval €€€ *Rambla del Raval 17–21, tel: 93-320 1490,* www.barcelo. com. A cutting-edge high-rise with panoramic views in the middle of El Raval, an indication of moves to smarten up this multicultural district once known as the Barri Xino. Wheelchair access and free Wi-Fi. 186 rooms.

Call € *Carrer de l'Arc de Sant Ramon del Call, tel: 93-302 1123,* www.ho telcall.es. This is a clean, small, air-conditioned 1-star hotel, located in the shady lanes of the Barri Gòtic. There's no bar or restaurant but everything you want is on your doorstep. 23 rooms.

Catalonia Portal de l'Àngel €€€ *Portal de l'Àngel 17, tel: 93-318 4141,* www.hoteles-catalonia.com. This charming hotel is housed in a stylish former palace on one of Barcelona's busiest pedestrian shopping streets, close to the Barri Gòtic, La Rambla and the Eixample. The 74 rooms are large and well-furnished, and there's a very pleasant garden patio. It's a good choice if you want to be in the thick of things. Wheelchair access.

Chic&basic Born €€–€€€ *Princesa 50, tel: 93-295 4652,* www.chicandbasic.com. This stylish, ultra-modern hotel is in a handsome 19th-century building, well located between the Ciutadella Park and the trendy Born area. Surprisingly good value. 31 rooms.

Chic&basic Zoo €€ *Passeig de Picasso 22, tel: 93-295 4652,* www.chicandbasic.com. A pleasant hotel, part of the Chic&basic chain, with 16 rooms and some stylish furnishings, close to the lively nightlife of El Born. It overlooks Ciutadella Park.

Colón €€€ *Avinguda de la Catedral 7, tel: 93-301 1404,* https://hotelcolonbarcelona.es. This is the closest you can get to the heart of the Barri Gòtic – right across the square from the cathedral. Sixth-floor rooms have large terraces; ask for one with a cathedral view if you book early. The Colón offers stylish furnishings and attention to detail in its 139 rooms and was once the home to Joan Miró.

Cuatro Naciones €€ *La Rambla 40, tel: 93-317 3624,* www.h4n.com. Long-established favourite on the lower half of La Rambla. This means night-time noise, but you're right in the heart of things and you get some great views. Wheelchair access. 54 rooms.

Hotel España €€€ *Carrer de Sant Pau 11, tel: 93-550 0000,* www.hotelespanya.com. Just off the lower part of La Rambla, the España may not be the place it once was, but it retains enough flavour of bygone days to recommend it. The beautiful public rooms were designed by *modernista* architect Domènech i Montaner. It brings modern chic to a 19th-century building. There are 82 comfortable rooms, an open air swimming pool, a spacious solarium, and a restaurant run by chef Martin Berasategui. Wheelchair access.

Gaudí €€ *Carrer de Nou de la Rambla 12, tel: 93-317 9032,* www.hotel gaudi.es. Situated opposite one of Gaudí's earliest works, the Palau Güell, and just off La Rambla, with 73 clean, comfortable, and simple rooms. Wheelchair access.

Gran Hotel Barcino €€ *Carrer de Jaume I, 6, tel: 93-302 2012,* www.hotel barcino.com. Just off the Plaça de Sant Jaume, right in the heart of the Barri Gòtic, this modern hotel is chic and well designed. The large, airy lobby outclasses the 61 rooms, though.

El Jardí €€ *Plaça Sant Josep Oriol 1, tel: 93-301 5900,* www.eljardi.com. Small hotel in the Barri Gòtic, overlooking two of the prettiest plazas in Barcelona. Jardí rooms are a bargain, although a plaza view costs a little more. 40 rooms. Free Wi-Fi and breakfast if you book directly.

Neri €€€€ *Carrer de Sant Sever 5, tel: 93-304 0655,* www.hotelneri.com. Elegant boutique hotel in a 17th-century palace overlooking one of the Barri Gòtic's most atmospheric squares, near the cathedral. The roof terrace has views over medieval spires. 22 rooms.

Nouvel Hotel €€€ *Carrer de Santa Ana 18–20, tel: 93-301 8274,* www. hotelnouvel.es. On a pedestrianised street between La Rambla and Portal d'Àngel, in an atmospheric area, this small hotel has a wonderful *modernista* lobby and dining room. The 78 rooms are plain, but well equipped.

Ohla €€€€ *Via Laietana 49, tel: 93-341 5050,* www.ohlaboutiquehotels. com. Opened in 2011, this 5-star hotel occupies a former department store. Behind its neoclassical facade are chic monochrome interiors. Highlights include a Michelin-star restaurant and rooftop deck with glass-sided pool. Wheelchair access. 74 rooms.

Oriente Atiram €€€ *Ramblas 45–47, tel: 93-302 2558,* www.atiramho tels.com. Nostalgic place located right on La Rambla. Built around a monastic complex, this was Barcelona's first official hotel. Ernest Hemingway and Hans Christian Andersen stayed here (but not together). Lots of character in spite of renovations. 147 rooms.

Peninsular €–€€ *Carrer de Sant Pau 34, tel: 93-302 3138,* www.hotelpen insular.net. Situated in an old Augustinian monastery, with rooms arranged around an inner courtyard. Friendly, helpful staff and good value for money. 59 rooms.

Rembrandt € *Carrer de Portaferrisa 23, tel: 93-318 1011,* www.hostal rembrandt.com. Clean, pleasant hostal though somewhat basic, the family-run Rembrandt is on a pedestrianised street just off La Rambla. Accommodation is up several flights of stairs and not all of the 31 rooms are en suite.

Rivoli Ramblas €€€€ *Rambla 128, tel: 93-481 7676,* www.hotelserhs rivolirambla.com. Busy hotel right on La Rambla with good facilities, including a pleasant restaurant, piano bar and a lovely terrace. The style in the 126 rooms ranges from Art Deco to Japanese. Rooms overlooking the courtyard at the back are quieter.

Roma Reial €€ *Plaça Reial 11, tel: 93-302 0366,* www.hotel-romareial. com. The accommodation is basic but the situation, in this buzzing square, makes it a good, cheap option for those who like to be where the action is. 52 rooms.

San Agusti €€ *Plaça Sant Agustí 3, tel: 93-318 1658,* www.hotelsa.com. A comfortable, traditional hotel with 77 rooms in a pretty little square near La Rambla. Wheelchair access.

Suizo €€€ *Plaça de l'Àngel 12, tel: 93-310 6108,* www.hotelsuizo.com. Close to the cathedral, and convenient for the Picasso Museum, this intimate, friendly hotel has a turn-of-the-20th-century air. 59 rooms.

EIXAMPLE

Alexandra Hotel €€–€€€ *Carrer de Mallorca 251, tel: 93-467 7166,* www. diagonalhotels.com. An excellent location for this business-like hotel between Rambla de Catalunya and Passeig de Gràcia. Enjoy the photography and 1950s and 1960s designer furniture. The 116 rooms are comfortable and nicely furnished. Wheelchair access.

Astoria Hotel €€€ *Carrer de París 203, tel: 93-209 8311,* www.derbyho tels.com. Part of the prestigious Derby chain, this sophisticated and quiet hotel is just a few paces from prime shopping territory on the Diagonal. Built in the 1950s, the Astoria is elegant and one of the best 3-star hotels in Spain. Some of the 117 rooms have small sitting rooms or garden terraces and there is a roof terrace with small pool.

Avenida Palace Hotel €€€€ *Gran Vía de les Corts Catalanes 605, tel: 93-301 9600,* www.avenidapalace.com. The place to stay if Barcelona's high-tech design craze seems too functional and cold. A luxurious, ornate hotel in the heart of the Eixample, on a busy thoroughfare. The 151 rooms and 2 suites are spacious and elegant. Wheelchair access.

Balmes Hotel €€€ *Carrer de Mallorca 216, tel: 93-445 6500,* www.derby hotels.com. Another Derby Hotel, the Balmes promises 'the advantages of the countryside in the heart of the city', and has an attractive leafy garden and a pool. Close to all the *modernista* masterpieces. It has a collection of African art and contemporary paintings. 98 rooms.

Hotel Casa Fuster €€€€ *Passeig de Gràcia, 132, tel: 93-255 3000,* www. hotelcasafuster.com. A sumptuous, 105-room hotel in a renovated Domènech i Montaner building complete with rooftop pool and views.

Catalonia Plaza Catalunya €€€ *Carrer de Bergara 11, tel: 93-301 5151,* www.hoteles-catalonia.com. A luxury, 4-star hotel just off Plaça de Catalunya, in a handsome 19th-century townhouse expanded to seven floors. The hotel has a relaxed but elegant feel, and service is top-notch, although the 150 rooms are small. Swimming pool in an inner courtyard. Wheelchair access.

Claris Hotel €€€€ *Carrer de Pau Claris 150, tel: 93-487 6262,* www.hotel claris.com. Another in the Derby chain, this is one of Barcelona's most elegant and expensive hotels, in the heart of the Eixample. Very high-tech design behind the facade of the Vedruna Palace and a guests-only museum of Egyptian art. The 124 rooms, many of which are split-level and even two-storey, exude cool chic, combining antiques and Catalan design. Small rooftop pool. Wheelchair access.

Condes de Barcelona Hotel €€€–€€€€ *Passeig de Gràcia 73, tel: 93-445 0000,* www.condesdebarcelona.com. With an ultra-chic address, just a block from Gaudí's La Pedrera, this popular hotel occupies two impressive former palaces on opposite corners. The 126 rooms are modern, large and elegant, decorated in bright colours. A favourite of architects and designers, as well as European and Japanese tourists, it boasts restaurant service overseen by Michelin-starred chef Martín Berasategui. Wheelchair access.

Silken Gran Havana €€€ *Gran Vía de les Corts Catalanes 647, tel: 93-341 7000,* www.hoteles-silken.com. A hip and high-tech hotel in an 1872 mansion with 145 rooms. Completely redecorated in 2017, it still showcases Barcelona's signature design elements in every detail. Panoramic roof terrace with pool. Wheelchair access.

Granvia €€€ *Gran Via de les Corts Catalanes 642, tel: 93-318 1900,* www.hotelgranvia.com. A small, intimate hotel with Old World style, occupying a 19th-century palace in a choice location, the Granvia has been operating since the 1930s. Fifty-three smallish but clean rooms, furnished with antiques. Good value. Offers parking and wheelchair access.

Majestic €€€€ *Passeig de Gràcia 68, tel: 93-488 1717,* www.hotelmajestic.es. The Majestic is a large, long-time favourite along one of the city's major shopping streets. An ever-changing menu can be found in the Restaurant Solc, while the Petit Comitè restaurant serves traditional Catalan cuisine. Spa. Wheelchair access. 275 rooms and suites.

Omm €€€€ *Rosselló 265, tel: 93-445 4000,* www.hotelomm.es. Just off Passeig de Gràcia, this award-winning designer hotel is for the chic and beautiful, or those who aspire to be. The 91 rooms are stylish and well lit, the rooftop pool is stunning with views of Gaudí's La Pedrera, and the in-house club is one of the best places to be for Barcelona's night scene. Wheelchair access.

El Palace €€€€ *Gran Via de les Corts Catalanes 668, tel: 93-510 1130,* www.hotelpalacebarcelona.com. A 1919 belle époque hotel, what used to be The Ritz is a classic place to stay. It's ultra-luxurious and grand, and situated on a splendid tree-lined avenue. Underwent a comprehensive refurbishment in 2017, it has competently fused a stylish update with the stunning features of the original building. Some of the 125 rooms have Roman-inspired bathrooms. Wheelchair access.

Regente €€€ *Rambla de Catalunya 76, tel: 93-487 5989*, www.hcchotels. es. A mid-sized hotel in a handsome 1913 *modernista* townhouse on La Rambla de Catalunya. The 79 rooms are simple, yet comfortable and there is a rooftop pool. Wheelchair access.

THE WATERFRONT

Hotel Arts €€€€ *Passeig de la Marina 19–21, tel: 93-221 1000*, www.hotel artsbarcelona.com. The Hotel Arts is a high-tech, deluxe high-rise, situated right on the beach in Vila Olímpica. Extremely efficient, and decorated with sophisticated, understated taste. Large rooms, huge bathrooms and amazing views of the Mediterranean and the city. Wheelchair access. 483 rooms.

Barcelona Princess €€€€ *Avinguda Diagonal 1, tel: 93-356 1000*, www. hotelbarcelonaprincess.com. Situated in the rejuvenated Diagonal Mar district, this cutting-edge hotel has stunning Mediterranean and city views. On the edge of the city but with good metro and tram connections. Good deals available out of season. 363 rooms.

W Barcelona €€€€ *Plaça Rosa dels Vents 1, tel: 93-295 2800*, www.w-barcelona.com. Rising high above the Mediterranean like a stylish beacon – all clean lines and designer chic – the W is in a good beach location, great for nightlife, although you may want a taxi to get into town. 473 rooms. Wheelchair access.

DIAGONAL

Hotel Rey Juan Carlos I €€€€ *Diagonal 661-671, tel: 93-364 4040*, www. fairmont.com/barcelona. Described as Barcelona's only 'urban resort hotel' it is also a premier business choice. Located at the west end of the Diagonal, it offers every amenity a demanding guest could want. Includes 432 rooms, several excellent restaurants, a swimming pool, gardens, fitness centre and spa. Wheelchair access.

DICTIONARY

ENGLISH–SPANISH

adj adjective   **adv** adverb   **BE** British English   **n** noun   **prep** preposition   **v** verb

A

abbey la abadía
accept v aceptar
access el acceso
accident el accidente
accommodation el alojamiento
account la cuenta
acupuncture la acupuntura
adapter el adaptador
address la dirección
admission la entrada
after después;
~**noon** la tarde;
~**shave** el bálsamo para después del afeitado
age la edad
agency la agencia
AIDS el sida
air el aire; ~ **conditioning** el aire acondicionado;
~ **pump** el aire; ~**line** la compañía aérea; ~**mail** el correo aéreo; ~**plane** el avión; ~**port** el aeropuerto
aisle el pasillo; ~ **seat** el asiento de pasillo
allergic alérgico; ~ **reaction** la reacción alérgica

allow v permitir
alone solo
alter v (clothing) hacer un arreglo
alternate route el otro camino
aluminum foil el papel de aluminio
amazing increíble
ambulance la ambulancia
American estadounidense
amusement park el parque de atracciones
anemic anémico
anesthesia la anestesia
animal el animal
ankle el tobillo
antibiotic el antibiótico
antiques store la tienda de -antigüedades
antiseptic cream la crema antiséptica
anything algo
apartment el apartamento
appendix (body part) el apéndice
appetizer el aperitivo
appointment la cita
arcade el salón de juegos recreativos

area code el prefijo
arm el brazo
aromatherapy la aromaterapia
around (the corner) doblando (la esquina)
arrivals (airport) las llegadas
arrive v llegar
artery la arteria
arthritis la artritis
arts las letras
Asian asiático
aspirin la aspirina
asthmatic asmático
ATM el cajero automático
attack el asalto
attend v asistir
attraction (place) el sitio de interés
attractive guapo
Australia Australia
Australian australiano
automatic automático;
~ **car** coche automático
available disponible

B

baby el bebé; ~ **bottle** el biberón;
~ **wipe** la toallita;
~**sitter** el/la canguro
back la espalda;

~**ache** el dolor de espalda; ~**pack** la mochila
bag la maleta
baggage el equipaje;
~ **claim** la recogida de equipajes; ~ **ticket** el talón de equipaje
bakery la panadería
ballet el ballet
bandage la tirita
bank el banco
bar el bar
barbecue la barbacoa
barber la peluquería de caballeros
baseball el béisbol
basket (grocery store) la cesta
basketball el baloncesto
bathroom el baño
battery (car) la batería
battery la pila
battleground el campo de batalla
be v ser, estar
beach la playa
beautiful precioso
bed la cama; ~ **and breakfast** la pensión
begin v empezar
before antes de

beginner principiante

behind detrás de

beige beis

belt el cinturón

berth la litera

best el/la mejor

better mejor

bicycle la bicicleta

big grande

bigger más grande

bike route el sendero para bicicletas

bikini el biquini; ~ **wax** la depilación de las ingles

bill v (charge) cobrar; ~ n (money) el billete; ~ n (of sale) el recibo

bird el pájaro

birthday el cumpleaños

black negro

bladder la vejiga

bland soso

blanket la manta

bleed v sangrar

blood la sangre; ~ **pressure** la tensión arterial

blouse la blusa

blue azul

board v embarcar

boarding pass la tarjeta de embarque

boat el barco

bone el hueso

book el libro; ~**store** la librería

boots las botas

boring aburrido

botanical garden el jardín botánico

bother v molestar

bottle la botella; ~ **opener** el abre-botellas

bowl el cuenco

box la caja

boxing match la pelea de boxeo

boy el niño; ~**friend** el novio

bra el sujetador

bracelet la pulsera

brakes (car) los frenos

break v romper

break-in (burglary) el allanamiento de morada

breakdown la avería

breakfast el desayuno

breast el seno; ~**feed** dar el pecho

breathe v respirar

bridge el puente

briefs (clothing) los calzoncillos

bring v traer

British británico

broken roto

brooch el broche

broom la escoba

brother el hermano

brown marrón

bug el insecto

building el edificio

burn v (CD) grabar

bus el autobús; ~ **station** la estación de autobuses; ~ **stop** la parada de autobús; ~ **ticket** el billete de autobús; ~ **tour** el recorrido en autobús

business los negocios; ~ **card** la tarjeta de negocios; ~ **cent-**

er el centro de negocios; ~ **class** la clase preferente; ~ **hours** el horario de atención al público

butcher el carnicero

buttocks las nalgas

buy v comprar

bye adiós

C

cabaret el cabaré

cabin (house) la cabaña; ~ **(ship)** el camarote

cable car el teleférico

cafe la cafetería

call v llamar; ~ n la llamada

calories las calorías

camera la cámara; **digital** ~ la cámara digital; ~ **case** la funda para la cámara; ~ **store** la tienda de fotografía

camp v acampar; ~ **stove** el hornillo; ~**site** el cámping

can opener el abrelatas

Canada Canadá

Canadian canadiense

cancel v cancelar

candy el caramelo

canned goods las conservas

canyon el cañón

car el coche; ~ **hire [BE]** el alquiler de coches; ~ **park [BE]** el aparcamiento; ~ **rental** el alquiler de coches; ~ **seat** el

asiento de niño

carafe la garrafa

card la tarjeta; **ATM** ~ la tarjeta de cajero automático; **credit** ~ la tarjeta de crédito; **debit** ~ la tarjeta de débito; **phone** ~ la tarjeta telefónica

carry-on (piece of hand luggage) el equipaje de mano

cart (grocery store) el carrito; ~ **(luggage)** el carrito para el equipaje

carton el cartón; ~ **of cigarettes** el cartón de tabaco

case (amount) la caja

cash v cobrar; ~ n el efectivo; ~ **advance** sacar dinero de la tarjeta

cashier el cajero

casino el casino

castle el castillo

cathedral la catedral

cave la cueva

CD el CD

cell phone el teléfono móvil

Celsius el grado centígrado

centimeter el centímetro

certificate el certificado

chair la silla; ~ **lift** la telesilla

change v (buses) cambiar; ~ n (money) el cambio

charcoal el carbón

charge v (credit card) cobrar; ~ n (cost) el precio

cheap barato

cheaper más barato

check v (on something) revisar; ~ v (luggage) facturar; ~ n (payment) el cheque; ~-in (airport) la facturación; ~-in (hotel) el registro; ~ing account la cuenta corriente; ~-out (hotel) la salida

Cheers! ¡Salud!

chemical toilet el váter químico

chemist [BE] la farmacia

cheque [BE] el cheque

chest (body part) el pecho; ~ pain el dolor de pecho

chewing gum el chicle

child el niño; ~ seat la silla para niños

children's menu el menú para niños

children's portion la ración para niños

Chinese chino

chopsticks los palillos chinos

church la iglesia

cigar el puro

cigarette el cigarrillo

class la clase; business ~ la clase preferente; economy ~ la clase económica; first ~ la primera

clase

classical music la música clásica

clean v limpiar; ~ adj limpio; ~ing product el producto de limpieza; ~ing supplies los productos de limpieza

clear v (on an ATM) borrar

cliff el acantilado

cling film [BE] el film transparente

close v (a shop) cerrar

closed cerrado

clothing la ropa; ~ store la tienda de ropa

club la discoteca

coat el abrigo

coffee shop la cafetería

coin la moneda

colander el escurridor

cold n (sickness) el catarro; ~ adj (temperature) frío

colleague el compañero de trabajo

cologne la colonia

color el color

comb el peine

come v venir

complaint la queja

computer el ordenador

concert el concierto; ~ hall la sala de conciertos

condition (medical) el estado de salud

conditioner el suavizante

condom el preservativo

conference la conferencia

confirm v confirmar

congestion la congestión

connect v (internet) conectarse

connection (internet) la conexión; ~ (flight) la conexión de vuelo

constipated estreñido

consulate el consulado

consultant el consultor

contact v ponerse en contacto con

contact lens la lentilla de contacto; ~ solution el líquido de lentillas de contacto

contagious contagioso

convention hall el salón de congresos

conveyor belt la cinta transportadora

cook v cocinar

cooking gas el gas butano

cool (temperature) frío

copper el cobre

corkscrew el sacacorchos

cost v costar

cot el catre

cotton el algodón

cough v toser; ~ n la tos

country code el código de país

cover charge la entrada

crash v (car) estrellarse

cream (ointment) la pomada

credit card la tarjeta de crédito

crew neck el cuello redondo

crib la cuna

crystal el cristal

cup la taza

currency la moneda; ~ exchange el cambio de divisas; ~ exchange office la casa de cambio

current account [BE] la cuenta corriente

customs las aduanas

cut v (hair) cortar; ~ n (injury) el corte

cute mono

cycling el ciclismo

D

damage v causar daño

damaged ha sufrido daños

dance v bailar; ~ club la discoteca

dangerous peligroso

dark oscuro

date (calendar) la fecha

day el día

deaf sordo

debit card la tarjeta de débito

deck chair la tumbona

declare v declarar

decline v (credit card) rechazar

deeply hondo

degrees (temperature) los grados

delay v retrasarse
delete v (**computer**) borrar
delicatessen la charcutería
delicious delicioso
denim tela vaquero
dentist el dentista
denture la dentadura
deodorant el desodorante
department store los grandes almacenes
departures (airport) las salidas
deposit v depositar; ~ n (**bank**) el depósito bancario; ~ v (**reserve a room**) la fianza
desert el desierto
dessert el postre
detergent el detergente
develop v (**film**) revelar
diabetic diabético
dial v marcar
diamond el diamante
diaper el pañal
diarrhea la diarrea
diesel el diesel
difficult difícil
digital digital; ~ **camera** la cámara digital; ~ **photos** las fotos digitales; ~ **prints** las fotos digitales
dining room el comedor
dinner la cena
direction la dirección
dirty sucio
disabled discapaci-

tado; ~ **accessible** [BE] el acceso para discapacitados
discharge (bodily fluid) la secreción
disconnect (computer) desconectar
discount el descuento
dish (kitchen) el plato; ~**washer** el lavavajillas; ~**washing liquid** el líquido lavavajillas
display v mostrar; ~ **case** la vitrina
disposable desechable; ~ **razor** la cuchilla desechable
dive v bucear
diving equipment el equipo de buceo
divorce v divorciar
dizzy mareado
doctor el médico
doll la muñeca
dollar (U.S.) el dólar
domestic nacional; ~ **flight** el vuelo nacional
door la puerta
dormitory el dormitorio
double bed la cama de matrimonio
downtown el centro
dozen la docena
drag lift el telesquí
dress (piece of clothing) el vestido; ~ **code** las normas de vestuario
drink v beber; ~ n la bebida; ~ **menu** la

carta de bebidas; ~**ing water** el agua potable
drive v conducir
driver's license number el número de permiso de conducir
drop (medicine) la gota
drowsiness la somnolencia
dry cleaner la tintorería
dubbed doblada
during durante
duty (tax) el impuesto; ~**free** libre de impuestos
DVD el DVD

E
ear la oreja; ~**ache** el dolor de oído
earlier más temprano
early temprano
earrings los pendientes
east el este
easy fácil
eat v comer
economy class la clase económica
elbow el codo
electric outlet el enchufe eléctrico
elevator el ascensor
e-mail v enviar un correo electrónico; ~ n el correo electrónico; ~ **address** la dirección de correo electrónico
emergency la emergencia; ~ **exit** la

salida de urgencia
empty v vaciar
enamel (jewelry) el esmalte
end v terminar
English el inglés
engrave v grabar
enjoy v disfrutar
enter v entrar
entertainment el entretenimiento
entrance la entrada
envelope el sobre
equipment el equipo
escalators las escaleras mecánicas
e-ticket el billete electrónico
EU resident el/la residente de la UE
euro el euro
evening la noche
excess el exceso
exchange v (**money**) cambiar; ~ v (**goods**) devolver; ~ n (**place**) la casa de cambio; ~ **rate** el tipo de cambio
excursion la excursión
excuse v (**to get past**) pedir perdón; ~ v (**to get attention**) disculparse
exhausted agotado
exit v salir; ~ n la salida
expensive caro
expert (skill level) experto
exposure (film) la foto
express rápido; ~ **bus** el autobús rápido; ~ **train** el

tren rápido

extension (phone) la extensión

extra adicional; **~ large** equis ele (XL)

extract v (tooth) extraer

eye el ojo

eyebrow wax la depilación de cejas

F

face la cara

facial la limpieza de cutis

family la familia

fan (appliance) el ventilador; **~ (souvenir)** el abanico

far lejos; **~-sighted** hipermétrope

farm la granja

fast rápido; **~ food** la comida rápida

faster más rápido

fat free sin grasa

father el padre

fax v enviar un fax; **~** n el fax; **~ number** el número de fax

fee la tasa

feed v alimentar

ferry el ferry

fever la fiebre

field (sports) el campo

fill v llenar ; **~ out** v (form) rellenar

filling (tooth) el empaste

film (camera) el carrete

fine (fee for breaking law) la multa

finger el dedo; **~nail** la uña del dedo

fire fuego; **~ department** los bomberos; **~ door** la puerta de incendios

first primero; **~ class** la primera clase

fit (clothing) quedar bien

fitting room el probador

fix v (repair) reparar

flashlight la linterna

flight el vuelo

floor el suelo

flower la flor

folk music la música folk

food la comida

foot el pie

football [BE] el fútbol

for para/por

forecast el pronóstico

forest el bosque

fork el tenedor

form el formulario

formula (baby) la fórmula infantil

fort el fuerte

fountain la fuente

free gratuito

freezer el congelador

fresh fresco

friend el amigo

frying pan la sartén

full completo; **~-service** el servicio completo; **~-time** a tiempo completo

G

game el partido

garage (parking) el garaje; **~ (repair)** el taller

garbage bag la bolsa de basura

gas la gasolina; **~ station** la gasolinera

gate (airport) la puerta

gay gay; **~ bar** el bar gay; **~ club** la discoteca gay

gel (hair) la gomina

get to v ir a

get off v (a train/bus/ subway) bajarse

gift el regalo; **~ shop** la tienda de regalos

girl la niña; **~friend** la novia

give v dar

glass (drinking) el vaso; **~ (material)** el vidrio

glasses las gafas

go v (somewhere) ir a

gold el oro

golf golf; **~ course** el campo de golf; **~ tournament** el torneo de golf

good n el producto; **~** adj bueno; **~ afternoon** buenas tardes; **~ evening** buenas noches; **~ morning** buenos días; **~bye** adiós

gram el gramo

grandchild el nieto

grandparent el abuelo

gray gris

green verde

grocery store el supermercado

ground la tierra; **~ floor** la planta baja; **~cloth** la tela impermeable

group el grupo

guide el guía; **~ book** la guía; **~ dog** el perro guía

gym el gimnasio

gynecologist el ginecólogo

H

hair el pelo; **~ dryer** el secador de pelo; **~ salon** la peluquería; **~brush** el cepillo de pelo; **~cut** el corte de pelo; **~spray** la laca, **~style** el peinado; **~stylist** el estilista

half medio; **~ hour** la media hora; **~-kilo** el medio kilo

hammer el martillo

hand la mano; **~ luggage [BE]** el equipaje de mano; **~bag [BE]** el bolso

handicapped discapacitado; **~-accessible** el acceso para discapacitados

hangover la resaca

happy feliz

hat el sombrero

have v tener

head (body part) la cabeza; **~ache** el dolor de cabeza; **~phones** los cascos

health la salud; **~ food store** la tienda de alimentos naturales

heart el corazón; **~ condition** padecer del corazón

heat v calentar; **~** n el calor

heater [heating BE] la calefacción

hello hola

helmet el casco

help v ayudar; **~** n la ayuda

here aquí

hi hola

high alto; **~chair** la trona; **~way** la autopista

hiking boots las botas de montaña

hill la colina

hire v **[BE]** alquilar; **~ car [BE]** el coche de alquiler

hitchhike v hacer autostop

hockey el hockey

holiday [BE] las vacaciones

horse track el hipódromo

hospital el hospital

hostel el albergue

hot (temperature) caliente; **~ (spicy)** picante; **~ spring** el agua termale; **~ water** el

agua caliente

hotel el hotel

hour la hora

house la casa; **~hold goods** los artículos para el hogar; **~keeping services** el servicio de limpieza de habitaciones

how (question) cómo; **~ much (question)** cuánto cuesta

hug v abrazar

hungry hambriento

hurt v **(have pain)** tener dolor

husband el marido

I

ibuprofen el ibuprofeno

ice el hielo; **~ hockey** el hockey sobre hielo

icy adj helado

identification el documento de identidad

ill v **(to feel)** encontrarse mal

in dentro

include v incluir

indoor pool la piscina cubierta

inexpensive barato

infected infectado

information (phone) el número de teléfono de información; **~ desk** el mostrador de información

insect el insecto; **~ bite** la picadura de

insecto; **~ repellent** el repelente de insectos

insert v introducir

insomnia el insomnio

instant message el mensaje instantáneo

insulin la insulina

insurance el seguro; **~ card** la tarjeta de seguro; **~ company** la compañía de seguros

interesting interesante

intermediate el nivel intermedio

international (airport area) internacional; **~ flight** el vuelo internacional; **~ student card** la tarjeta internacional de estudiante

internet la internet; **~ cafe** el cibercafé; **~ service** el servicio de internet; **wireless ~** el acceso inalámbrico

interpreter el/la intérprete

intersection el cruce

intestine el intestino

introduce v presentar

invoice [BE] la factura

Ireland Irlanda

Irish irlandés

iron v planchar; **~** n **(clothes)** la plancha

Italian italiano

J

jacket la chaqueta

jar el bote

jaw la mandíbula

jazz el jazz; **~ club** el club de jazz

jeans los vaqueros

jet ski la moto acuática

jeweler la joyería

jewelry las joyas

join v acompañar a

joint (body part) la articulación

K

key la llave; **~ card** la llave electrónica; **~ ring** el llavero

kiddie pool la piscina infantil

kidney (body part) el riñón

kilo el kilo; **~gram** el kilogramo; **~meter** el kilómetro

kiss v besar

kitchen la cocina; **~ foil [BE]** el papel de aluminio

knee la rodilla

knife el cuchillo

L

lace el encaje

lactose intolerant alérgico a la lactosa

lake el lago

large grande; **~er** más grande

last último

late (time) tarde; **~er** más tarde

launderette [BE] la lavandería

laundromat la lavandería

laundry la colada; **~ facility** la lavandería; **~ service** el servicio de lavandería
lawyer el abogado
leather el cuero
to leave v salir
left (direction) la izquierda
leg la pierna
lens la lente
less menos
lesson la lección
letter la carta
library la biblioteca
life la vida; **~ jacket** el chaleco salvavidas; **~guard** el socorrista
lift n [BE] el ascensor; **~** v **(to give a ride)** llevar en coche; **~ pass** el pase de acceso a los remontes
light n **(overhead)** la luz; **~** v **(cigarette)** dar fuego; **~bulb** la bombilla
lighter el mechero
like v gustar; **I like me gusta**
line (train) la línea
linen el lino
lip el labio
liquor store la tienda de bebidas alcohólicas
liter el litro
little pequeño
live v vivir
liver (body part) el hígado
loafers los mocasines

local de la zona
lock v cerrar; **~** n el cerrojo
locker la taquilla
log on v **(computer)** iniciar sesión
log off v **(computer)** cerrar sesión
long largo; **~ sleeves** las mangas largas; **~-sighted** [BE] hipermétrope
look v mirar
lose v **(something)** perder
lost perdido; **~ and found** la oficina de objetos perdidos
lotion la crema hidratante
louder más alto
love v querer; **~** n el amor
low bajo; **~er** más bajo
luggage el equipaje; **~ cart** el carrito de equipaje; **~ locker** la consigna automática; **~ ticket** el talón de equipaje; **hand ~** [BE] el equipaje de mano
lunch la comida
lung el pulmón

M

magazine la revista
magnificent magnífico
mail v enviar por correo; **~** n el correo; **~box** el buzón de correo
main principal; **~**

attractions los principales sitios de interés; **~ course** el plato principal
make up a prescription v [BE] despachar medicamentos
mall el centro comercial
man el hombre
manager el gerente
manicure la manicura
manual car el coche con transmisión manual
map el mapa
market el mercado
married casado
marry v casarse
mass (church service) la misa
massage el masaje
match la cerilla
meal la comida
measure v **(someone)** medir
measuring cup la taza medidora
measuring spoon la cuchara medidora
mechanic el mecánico
medicine el medicamento
medium (size) mediano
meet v **(someone)** conocer
meeting la reunión; **~ room** la sala de reuniones
membership card la tarjeta de socio

memorial (place) el monumento conmemorativo
memory card la tarjeta de memoria
mend v zurcir
menstrual cramps los dolores menstruales
menu la carta
message el mensaje
meter (parking) el parquímetro
microwave el microondas
midday [BE] el mediodía
midnight la medianoche
mileage el kilometraje
mini-bar el minibar
minute el minuto
missing desaparecido
mistake el error
mobile móvil; **~ home** la caravana; **~ phone** [BE] el teléfono móvil
mobility la movilidad
money el dinero
month el mes
mop la fregona
moped el ciclomotor
more más
morning la mañana
mosque la mezquita
mother la madre
motion sickness el mareo
motor el motor; **~ boat** la lancha motora; **~cycle** la motocicleta; **~way** [BE] la autopista

mountain la montaña;
~ **bike** la bicicleta
de montaña
mousse (hair) la
espuma para el pelo
mouth *n* la boca
movie la película; ~
theater el cine
mug *v* asaltar
muscle (body part) el
músculo
museum el museo
music la música; ~
store la tienda de
música

N

nail la uña; ~ **file** la
lima de uñas; ~
salon el salon de
manicura
name el nombre
napkin la servilleta
nappy [BE] el pañale
nationality la
nacionalidad
nature preserve la
reserva natural
(be) nauseous *v* tener
náuseas
near cerca;
~-**sighted** miope;
~**by** cerca de aquí
neck el cuello
necklace el collar
need *v* necesitar
newspaper el
periódico
newsstand el quiosco
next próximo
nice *adj* amable
night la noche; ~**club**
la discoteca
no no

non sin; ~-**alco-
holic** sin alcohol;
~-**smoking** para no
fumadores
noon el mediodía
north el norte
nose la nariz
note [BE] el billete
nothing nada
notify *v* avisar
**novice (skill
level)** principiante
now ahora
number el número
nurse el enfermero/la
enfermera

O

office la oficina; ~
hours (doctor's) las
horas de consulta;
~ **hours (other of-
fices)** el horario de
oficina
off-licence [BE] la
tienda de bebidas
alcohólicas
oil el aceite
OK de acuerdo
old *adj* viejo
on the corner en la
esquina
once una vez
one uno; ~-**way
ticket** el billete
de ida; ~-**way
street** la calle de
sentido único
only solamente
open *v* abrir; ~ *adj*
abierto
opera la ópera; ~
house el teatro de
la ópera

opposite frente a
optician el oculista
orange (color) naranja
orchestra la orquesta
order *v* pedir
outdoor pool la
piscina exterior
outside fuera
over sobre; ~
**the counter
(medication)** sin
receta; ~**look
(scenic place)** el
mirador; ~**night** por
la noche
oxygen treatment
la oxigenoterapia

P

p.m. de la tarde
pacifier el chupete
pack *v* hacer las
maletas
package el paquete
paddling pool [BE] la
piscina infantil
pad [BE] la compresa
pain el dolor
pajamas los pijamas
palace el palacio
pants los pantalones
pantyhose las medias
paper el papel; ~
towel el papel de
cocina
paracetamol [BE] el
paracetamol
park *v* aparcar;
~ *n* el parque;
~**ing garage** el
párking; ~**ing lot** el
aparcamiento
**parliament build-
ing** el palacio de las

cortes
part (for car) la pieza;
~-**time** a tiempo
parcial
pass through *v* estar
de paso
passenger el pasajero
passport el pasaporte;
~-**control** el control
de pasaportes
password la
contraseña
pastry shop la
pastelería
path el camino
pay *v* pagar; ~
phone el teléfono
público
**peak (of a moun-
tain)** la cima
pearl la perla
pedestrian el peatón
pediatrician el
pediatra
pedicure la pedicura
pen el bolígrafo
penicillin la penicilina
penis el pene
per por; ~ **day** por
día; ~ **hour** por
hora; ~ **night** por
noche; ~ **week** por
semana
perfume el perfume
period (menstrual) la
regla; ~ **(of time)** la
época
permit *v* permitir
petite las tallas
pequeñas
petrol la gasolina; ~
station la gaso-
linera
pewter el peltre

pharmacy la farmacia
phone v
 hacer una llamada;
 ~ n el teléfono; ~
 call la llamada de
 teléfono; ~ **card** la
 tarjeta telefónica; ~
 number el número
 de teléfono
photo la foto;
 ~**copy** la fotocopia;
 ~**graphy** la foto-
 grafía
pick up v (some-
 thing) recoger
picnic area la zona
 para picnic
piece el trozo
Pill (birth control) la
 píldora
pillow la almohada
**personal identifica-
 tion number
 (PIN)** la clave
pink rosa
piste [BE] la pista; ~
 map [BE] el mapa
 de pistas
pizzeria la pizzería
place v (a bet) hacer
 una apuesta
plane el avión
plastic wrap el film
 transparente
plate el plato
platform [BE]
 (train) el andén
platinum el platino
play v jugar; ~ n
 (theater) la obra de
 teatro; ~**ground** el
 patio de recreo;
 ~**pen** el parque
please por favor

pleasure el placer
plunger el desa-
 tascador
plus size la talla
 grande
pocket el bolsillo
poison el veneno
poles (skiing) los
 bastones
police la policía; ~
 report el certificado
 de la policía; ~ **sta-
 tion** la comisaría
pond el estanque
pool la piscina
pop music la música
 pop
portion la ración
post [BE] el correo;
 ~ **office** la oficina
 de correos; ~**box
 [BE]** el buzón de
 correos; ~**card** la
 tarjeta postal
pot la olla
pottery la cerámica
**pounds (British
 sterling)** las libras
 esterlinas
pregnant embarazada
prescribe v recetar
prescription la receta
press v (cloth-
 ing) planchar
price el precio
print v imprimir
problem el problema
produce las frutas y
 verduras; ~ **store** la
 frutería y verdulería
prohibit v prohibir
pronounce v
 pronunciar
public el público

pull v (door sign) tirar
purple morado
purse el bolso
push v (door
 sign) empujar;
 ~**chair [BE]** el
 cochecito de niño

Q

quality n la calidad
question la pregunta
quiet adj tranquilo

R

racetrack el circuito
 de carreras
racket (sports) la
 raqueta
**railway station
 [BE]** la estación de
 trenes
rain la lluvia;
 ~**coat** el chubas-
 quero; ~**forest** el
 bosque pluvial;
 ~**y** adj lluvioso
rap (music) el rap
rape v violar; ~ n la
 violación
rash la erupción
 cutánea
razor blade la hoja de
 afeitar
reach v localizar
ready listo
real auténtico
receipt el recibo
receive v recibir
reception la recepción
recharge v recargar
recommend v
 recomendar
recommendation la
 recomendación

recycle v reciclar
red rojo
refrigerator n la
 nevera
region la región
registered mail el
 correo certificado
regular normal
relationship la
 relación
rent v alquilar
rental car el coche de
 alquiler
repair v arreglar
repeat v repetir
reservation la reserva;
 ~ **desk** la taquilla
reserve v reservar
restaurant el
 restaurante
restroom el servicio
retired jubilado
return v (some-
 thing) devolver; ~ n
 [BE] la ida y vuelta
rib (body part) la
 costilla
right (direction) derecha; ~ **of way** prior-
 idad de paso
ring el anillo
river n el río
road map el mapa de
 carreteras
rob v atracar
robbed atracado
romantic romántico
room la habitación;
 ~ **key** la llave de
 habitación; ~ **ser-
 vice** el servicio de
 habitaciones
round-trip ida y vuelta
route la ruta

rowboat la barca de remos
rubbish [BE] la basura; **~ bag [BE]** la bolsa de basura
rugby el rugby
ruins las ruinas
rush la prisa

S

sad triste
safe *n* la caja fuerte; **~** *adj* seguro
sales tax el IVA
same mismo
sandals las sandalias
sanitary napkin la compresa
saucepan el cazo
sauna la sauna
save *v* **(computer)** guardar
savings (account) la cuenta de ahorro
scanner el escáner
scarf la bufanda
schedule *v* programar; **~** *n* el horario
school el colegio
science la ciencia
scissors las tijeras
sea el mar
seat el asiento
security la seguridad
see *v* ver
self-service el autoservicio
sell *v* vender
seminar el seminario
send *v* enviar
senior citizen jubilado
separated (marriage) -separado
serious serio

service (in a restaurant) el servicio
sexually transmitted disease (STD) la enfermedad de transmisión sexual
shampoo el champú
sharp afilado
shaving cream la crema de afeitar
sheet la sábana
ship *v* enviar
shirt la camisa
shoe store la zapatería
shoes los zapatos
shop *v* comprar
shopping ir de compras; **~ area** la zona de compras; **~ centre [BE]** el centro comercial; **~ mall** el centro comercial
short corto; **~ sleeves** las mangas cortas; **~s** los pantalones cortos; **~-sighted [BE]** miope
shoulder el hombro
show *v* enseñar
shower la ducha
shrine el santuario
sick enfermo
side el lado; **~ dish** la guarnición; **~ effect** el efecto secundario; **~ order** la guarnición
sightsee *v* hacer turismo
sightseeing tour el recorrido turístico
sign *v* **(name)** firmar
silk la seda

silver la plata
single (unmarried) soltero; **~ bed** la cama; **~ prints** una copia; **~ room** una habitación individual
sink el lavabo
sister la hermana
sit *v* sentarse
size la talla
skin la piel
skirt la falda
ski *v* esquiar; **~** *n* el esquí; **~ lift** el telesquí
sleep *v* dormir; **~er car** el coche cama; **~ing bag** el saco de dormir
slice *v* cortar en rodajas
slippers las zapatillas
slower más despacio
slowly despacio
small pequeño
smaller más pequeño
smoke *v* fumar
smoking (area) la zona de fumadores
snack bar la cafetería
sneakers las zapatillas de deporte
snorkeling equipment el equipo de esnórquel
snow la nieve; **~board** la tabla de snowboard; **~shoe** la raqueta de nieve; **~y** nevado
soap el jabón
soccer el fútbol
sock el calcetín

some alguno
soother [BE] el chupete
sore throat las anginas
sorry lo siento
south el sur
souvenir el recuerdo; **~ store** la tienda de recuerdos
spa el centro de salud y belleza
Spain España
Spanish el español
spatula la espátula
speak *v* hablar
special (food) la especialidad de la casa
specialist (doctor) el especialista
specimen el ejemplar
speeding el exceso de velocidad
spell *v* deletrear
spicy picante
spine (body part) la columna vertebral
spoon la cuchara
sports los deportes; **~ massage** el masaje deportivo
sporting goods store la tienda de deportes
sprain el esguince
square cuadrado; **~ kilometer** el kilómetro cuadrado; **~ meter** el metro cuadrado
stadium el estadio
stairs las escaleras
stamp *v* **(a**

ticket) picar;
~ n (postage) el
sello

start v empezar

starter [BE] el
aperitivo

station la estación;
bus ~ la estación
de autobuses; gas
~ la gasolinera;
muster ~ [BE] el
punto de reunión;
petrol ~ [BE] la
gasolinera; subway
~ el metro; train
~ la estación de tren

statue la estatua

stay v quedarse

steal v robar

steep empinado

sterling silver la
plata esterlina

sting el escozor

stolen robado

stomach el estómago;
~ache el dolor de
estómago

stop v pararse; ~ n la
parada

storey [BE] la planta

stove el horno

straight recto

strange extraño

stream el arroyo

stroller el cochecito

student el estudiante

study v estudiar

stunning impresio-
nante

subtitle el subtítulo

subway el metro; ~
station la estación
de metro

suit el traje

suitcase la maleta

sun el sol; ~block el
protector solar total;
~burn la quemadura
solar; ~glasses las
gafas de sol;
~ny soleado;
~screen el protec-
tor solar; ~stroke
la insolación

super (fuel) súper;
~market el super-
mercado

surfboard la tabla
de surf

surgical spirit [BE] el
alcohol etílico

swallow v tragar

sweater el jersey

sweatshirt la
sudadera

sweet (taste) dulce;
~s [BE] los cara-
melos

swelling la hinchazón

swim v nadar;
~suit el bañador

symbol (keyboard) el
símbolo

synagogue la
sinagoga

T

table la mesa

tablet (medicine) el
comprimido

take v llevar; ~ away
[BE] para llevar

tampon el tampón

tapas bar el bar de
tapas

taste v probar

taxi el taxi

team el equipo

telephone el teléfono

temporary provisional

tennis el tenis

tent la tienda de
campaña; ~ peg la
estaca; ~ pole el
mástil

terminal (airport) la
terminal

terracotta la ter-
racotta

terrible terrible

text v (send a
message) enviar
un mensaje de texto;
~ n (message) el
texto

thank v dar las gracias
a; ~ you gracias

that eso

theater el teatro

there ahí

thief el ladrón

thigh el muslo

thirsty sediento

this esto

throat la garganta

ticket el billete; ~
office el despacho
de billetes; ~ed pas-
senger el pasajero
con billete

tie (clothing) la
corbata

time el tiempo; ~table
[BE] el horario

tire la rueda

tired cansado

tissue el pañuelo de
paper

tobacconist el
estanco

today hoy

toe el dedo del pie;

~nail la uña del
pie

toilet [BE] el servicio;
~ paper el papel
higiénico

tomorrow mañana

tongue la lengua

tonight esta noche

too demasiado

tooth el diente;
~brush el cepillo de
dientes; ~paste la
pasta de dientes

total (amount) el
total

tough (food) duro

tourist el turista; ~ in-
formation office la
oficina de turismo

tour el recorrido
turístico

tow truck la grúa

towel la toalla

tower la torre

town la ciudad; ~ hall
el ayuntamiento; ~
map el mapa de
ciudad; ~ square la
plaza

toy el juguete; ~
store la tienda de
juguetes

track (train) el
andén

traditional tradicional

traffic light el
semáforo

trail la pista; ~
map el mapa de
la pista

trailer el remolque

train el tren; ~
station la estación
de tren

transfer v cambiar
translate v traducir
trash la basura
travel v viajar; ~ **agency** la agencia de viajes; ~ **sickness** el mareo; **~er's check [cheque BE]** el cheque de viaje
tree el árbol
trim (hair cut) cortarse las puntas
trip el viaje
trolley [BE] el carrito
trousers [BE] los pantalones
T-shirt la camiseta
turn off v apagar
turn on v encender
TV la televisión
type v escribir a máquina
tyre [BE] la rueda

U

United Kingdom (U.K.) el Reino Unido
United States (U.S.) los Estados Unidos
ugly feo
umbrella el paraguas
unattended desatendido
unconscious inconsciente
underground [BE] el metro; ~ **station [BE]** la estación de metro
underpants [BE] los calzoncillos

understand v entender
underwear la ropa interior
university la universidad
unleaded (gas) la gasolina sin plomo
upper superior
urgent urgente
use v usar
username el nombre de usuario
utensil el cubierto

V

vacancy la habitación libre
vacation las vacaciones
vaccination la vacuna
vacuum cleaner la aspiradora
vaginal infection la infección vaginal
valid validez
valley el valle
valuable valioso
VAT [BE] el IVA
vegetarian vegetariano
vehicle registration el registro del coche
viewpoint [BE] el mirador
village el pueblo
vineyard la viña
visa (passport document) el visado
visit v visitar; **~ing hours** el horario de visita
visually impaired la persona con

discapacidad visual
vitamin la vitamina
V-neck el cuello de pico
vomit v vomitar

W

wait v esperar; ~ n la espera; **~ing room** la sala de espera
waiter el camarero
waitress la camarera
wake v despertarse; **~-up call** la llamada despertador
walk v caminar; ~ n la caminata; **~ing route** la ruta de senderismo
wallet la cartera
warm v (something) calentar; ~ adj (temperature) calor
washing machine la lavadora
watch el reloj
waterfall la cascada
weather el tiempo
week la semana; **~end** el fin de semana; **~ly** semanal
welcome v acoger
well bien; **~-rested** descansado
west el oeste
what (question) qué
wheelchair la silla de ruedas; ~ **ramp** la rampa para silla de ruedas
when (question) cuándo

where (question) dónde
white blanco; ~ **gold** el oro blanco
who (question) quién
widowed viudo
wife la mujer
window la ventana; ~ **case** el escaparate
windsurfer el surfista
wine list la carta de vinos
wireless inalámbrico; ~ **internet** el acceso inalámbrico a internet; ~ **internet service** el servicio inalámbrico a internet; ~ **phone** el teléfono móvil
with con
withdraw v retirar; **~al (bank)** retirar fondos
without sin
woman la mujer
wool la lana
work v trabajar
wrap v envolver
wrist la muñeca
write v escribir

Y

year el año
yellow amarillo
yes sí
yesterday ayer
young joven
youth hostel el albergue juvenil

Z

zoo el zoológico

SPANISH–ENGLISH

A

a tiempo completo full-time

a tiempo parcial part-time

la abadía abbey

el abanico fan (souvenir)

abierto adj open

el abogado lawyer

abrazar v hug

el abrebotellas bottle opener

el abrelatas can opener

el abrigo coat

abrir v open

el abuelo grandparent

aburrido boring

acampar v camp

el acantilado cliff

el acceso access; **~ inalámbrico a internet** wireless internet; **~ para discapacitados** handicapped- [disabled- BE] accessible

el accidente accident

el aceite oil

aceptar v accept

acoger v welcome

acompañar a v join

la acupuntura acupuncture

el adaptador adapter

adicional extra

adiós goodbye

las aduanas customs

el aeropuerto airport

afilado sharp

la agencia agency; **~ de viajes** travel agency

agotado exhausted

el agua water; **~ caliente** hot water; **~ potable** drinking water

las aguas termales hot spring

ahí there

ahora now

el aire air, air pump; **~ acondicionado** air conditioning

el albergue hostel; **~ juvenil** youth hostel

alérgico allergic; **~ a la lactosa** lactose intolerant

algo anything

el algodón cotton

alguno some

alimentar v feed

el allanamiento de morada break-in (burglary)

la almohada pillow

el alojamiento accommodation

alquilar v rent [hire BE]; **el ~ de coches** car rental [hire BE]

alto high

amable nice

amarillo yellow

la ambulancia ambulance

el amigo friend

el amor n love

el andén track [platform BE] (train)

anémico anemic

la anestesia anesthesia

las anginas sore throat

el anillo ring

el animal animal

antes de before

el antibiótico antibiotic

el año year

apagar v turn off

el aparcamiento parking lot [car park BE]

aparcar v park

el apartamento apartment

el apéndice appendix (body part)

el aperitivo appetizer [starter BE]

aquí here

el árbol tree

la aromaterapia aromatherapy

arreglar v repair

el arroyo stream

la arteria artery

la articulación joint (body part)

los artículos goods; **~ para el hogar** household good

la artritis arthritis

asaltar v mug

el asalto attack

el ascensor elevator [lift BE]

asiático Asian

el asiento seat; **~ de niño** car seat; **~ de pasillo** aisle seat

asistir v attend

asmático asthmatic

la aspiradora vacuum cleaner

la aspirina aspirin

atracado robbed

atracar v rob

Australia Australia

australiano Australian

auténtico real

el autobús bus; **~ rápido** express bus

automático automatic

la autopista highway [motorway BE]

el autoservicio self-service

la avería breakdown

el avión airplane, plane

avisar v notify

ayer yesterday

la ayuda n help

ayudar v help

el ayuntamiento town hall

azul blue

B

bailar v dance

bajarse v get off (a train, bus, subway)

bajo low
el ballet ballet
el baloncesto basketball
el bálsamo para después del afeitado aftershave
el banco bank
el bañador swimsuit
el baño bathroom
el bar bar; **~ de tapas** tapas bar; **~ gay** gay bar
barato cheap, inexpensive
la barbacoa barbecue
la barca de remos rowboat
el barco boat
los bastones poles (skiing)
la basura trash [rubbish BE]
la batería battery (car)
el bebé baby
beber v drink
la bebida n drink
beis beige
el béisbol baseball
besar v kiss
el biberón baby bottle
la biblioteca library
la bicicleta bicycle; **~ de montaña** mountain bike
el billete n bill (money); **~** ticket; **~ de autobús** bus ticket; **~ de ida** one-way (ticket); **~ de ida y vuelta** round trip (return BE); **~ electrónico** e-ticket

el biquini bikini
blanco white
la blusa blouse
la boca mouth
el bolígrafo pen
la bolsa de basura garbage [rubbish BE] bag
el bolsillo pocket
el bolso purse [handbag BE]
los bomberos fire department
la bombilla lightbulb
borrar v clear (on an ATM); **~** v delete (computer)
el bosque forest; **~ pluvial** rainforest
las botas boots; **~ de montaña** hiking boots
el bote jar
la botella bottle
el brazo arm
británico British
el broche brooch
bucear to dive
bueno adj good
buenas noches good evening
buenas tardes good afternoon
buenos días good morning
la bufanda scarf
el buzón de correo mailbox [postbox BE]

C

la cabaña cabin (house)
el cabaré cabaret

la cabeza head (body part)
la cafetería cafe, coffee shop, snack bar
la caja case (amount); **~ fuerte** n safe
el cajero cashier; **~ automático** ATM
el calcetín sock
la calefacción heater [heating BE]
calentar v heat, warm
la calidad quality
la calle de sentido único one-way street
calor hot, warm (temperature)
las calorías calories
los calzoncillos briefs [underpants BE] (clothing)
la cama single bed; **~ de matrimonio** double bed
la cámara camera; **~ digital** digital camera
la camarera waitress
el camarero waiter
el camarote cabin (ship)
cambiar v change, exchange, transfer
el cambio n change (money); **~ de divisas** currency exchange
caminar v walk
la caminata n walk
el camino path
la camisa shirt
la camiseta T-shirt
el cámping campsite

el campo field (sports); **~ de batalla** battleground; **~ de golf** golf course
Canadá Canada
canadiense Canadian
cancelar v cancel
el/la canguro babysitter
cansado tired
el cañón canyon
la cara face
los caramelos candy [sweets BE]
la caravana mobile home
el carbón charcoal
el carnicero butcher
caro expensive
el carrete film (camera)
el carrito cart [trolley BE] (grocery store); **~ de equipaje** luggage cart
la carta letter
la carta n menu; **~ de bebidas** drink menu; **~ para niños** children's menu; **~ de vinos** wine list
la cartera n wallet
el cartón carton; **~ de tabaco** carton of cigarettes
la casa house; **~ de cambio** currency exchange office
casado married
casarse v marry
la cascada waterfall
el casco helmet

los cascos headphones
el casino casino
el castillo castle
el catarro cold (sickness)
la catedral cathedral
el catre cot
causar daño v damage
el cazo saucepan
el CD CD
la cena dinner
el centímetro centimeter
el centro downtown area; ~ **comercial** shopping mall [centre BE]; ~ **de negocios** business center; ~ **de salud y belleza** spa
el cepillo de pelo hair brush
la cerámica pottery
cerca near; ~ **de aquí** nearby
la cerilla n match
cerrado closed
cerrar v close, lock; ~ **sesión** v log off (computer)
el cerrojo n lock
el certificado certificate; ~ **de la policía** police report
la cesta basket (grocery store)
el chaleco salvavidas life jacket
el champú shampoo
la chaqueta jacket
la charcutería delicatessen

el cheque n check [cheque BE] (payment); ~ **de viaje** traveler's check [cheque BE]
el chicle chewing gum
chino Chinese
el chubasquero raincoat
el chupete pacifier [soother BE]
el cibercafé internet cafe
el ciclismo cycling
el ciclomotor moped
la ciencia science
el cigarrillo cigarette
la cima peak (of a mountain)
el cine movie theater
la cinta transportadora conveyor belt
el cinturón n belt
el circuito de carreras racetrack
la cita appointment
la ciudad town
la clase class; ~ **económica** economy class; ~ **preferente** business class
la clave personal identification number (PIN)
el club de jazz jazz club
cobrar v bill (charge); ~ v cash; ~ v charge (credit card)
el cobre copper
el coche n car; ~ **de alquiler** rental [hire BE] car; ~ **automáti-**

co automatic car; ~ **cama** sleeper [sleeping BE] car; ~ **con transmisión manual** manual car
el cochecito stroller [pushchair BE]
la cocina kitchen
cocinar v cook
el código de país country code
el codo elbow
la colada laundry
el colegio school
la colina hill
el collar necklace
la colonia cologne
el color color
la columna vertebral spine (body part)
el comedor dining room
comer v eat
la comida food, lunch, meal; ~ **rápida** fast food
la comisaría police station
cómo how
el compañero de trabajo colleague
la compañía company; ~ **aérea** airline; ~ **de seguros** insurance company
comprar v buy, shop
la compresa sanitary napkin [pad BE]
el comprimido tablet (medicine)
con with; ~ **plomo** leaded (gas)
el concierto concert

conducir v drive
conectarse v connect (internet)
la conexión connection (internet); ~ **de vuelo** connection (flight)
la conferencia conference
confirmar v confirm
el congelador freezer
la congestión congestion
conocer v meet (someone)
la consigna automática luggage locker
el consulado Consulate
el consultor consultant
contagioso contagious
la contraseña password
el control de pasaportes passport control
el corazón heart
la corbata tie (clothing)
el correo n mail [post BE]; ~ **aéreo** airmail; ~ **certificado** registered mail; ~ **electrónico** n e-mail
cortar v cut (hair); ~ **en rodajas** to slice
cortarse las puntas v trim (hair cut)
el corte n cut (injury); ~ **de pelo** haircut
corto short

costar v cost

la costilla rib (body part)

la crema cream; ~ **antiséptica** antiseptic cream; ~ **de afeitar** shaving cream; ~ **hidratante** lotion

el cristal crystal

el cruce intersection

cuándo when (question)

cuánto cuesta how much

el cubierto utensil

la cuchara spoon; ~ **medidora** measuring spoon

la cucharadita teaspoon

la cuchilla desechable disposable razor

el cuchillo knife

el cuello neck; ~ **de pico** V-neck; ~ **redondo** crew neck

el cuenco bowl

la cuenta account; ~ **de ahorro** savings account; ~ **corriente** checking [current BE] account

cuero leather

la cueva cave

el cumpleaños birthday

la cuna crib

D

dar to give; ~ **el pecho** breastfeed; ~ **fuego** light (ciga-

rette); ~ **las gracias a** v thank

de from, of; ~ **acuerdo** OK; ~ **la mañana** a.m.; ~ **la tarde** p.m.; ~ **la zona** local

declarar v declare

el dedo finger; ~ **del pie** toe

deletrear v spell

delicioso delicious

la dentadura denture

el dentista dentist

dentro in

la depilacion wax; ~ **de cejas** eyebrow wax; ~ **de las ingles** bikini wax

deportes sports

depositar v deposit

el depósito bancario deposit (bank)

la derecha right (direction)

desaparecido missing

el desatascador plunger

desatendido unattended

el desayuno breakfast

descansado well-rested

desconectar v disconnect (computer)

el descuento discount

desechable disposable

el desierto desert

el desodorante deodorant

despachar medicamentos v fill [make up BE] a prescription

el despacho de billetes ticket office

despacio slowly

despertarse v wake

después after

el detergente detergent

detrás de behind (direction)

devolver v exchange, return (goods)

el día day

diabético diabetic

el diamante diamond

la diarrea diarrhea

el diente tooth

el diesel diesel

difícil difficult

digital digital

el dinero money

la dirección direction

la dirección address; ~ **de correo electrónico** e-mail address

discapacitado handicapped [disabled BE]

la discoteca club (dance, night); ~ **gay** gay club

disculparse v excuse (to get attention)

disfrutar v enjoy

disponible available

divorciar v divorce

doblada dubbed

doblando (la esquina) around (the corner)

la docena dozen

el documento de identidad identification

el dólar dollar (U.S.)

el dolor pain; ~ **de cabeza** headache; ~ **de espalda** backache; ~ **de estómago** stomachache; ~ **de oído** earache; ~ **de pecho** chest pain

los dolores menstruales menstrual cramps

dónde where (question)

dormir v sleep

el dormitorio dormitory

la ducha shower

dulce sweet (taste)

durante during

el DVD DVD

E

la edad age

el edificio building

el efectivo cash

el efecto secundario side effect

el ejemplar specimen

embarazada pregnant

embarcar v board

la emergencia emergency

el empaste filling (tooth)

empezar v begin, start

empinado steep

empujar v push (door sign)

en la esquina on the corner

el encaje lace

encender v turn on

el enchufe eléctrico electric outlet

encontrarse mal v be ill

la enfermedad de transmisión sexual sexually transmitted disease (STD)

el enfermero/la enfermera nurse

enfermo sick

enseñar v show

entender v understand

la entrada admission/cover charge; ~ entrance

entrar v enter

el entretenimiento entertainment

enviar v send, ship; ~ **por correo** v mail; ~ **un correo electrónico** v e-mail; ~ **un fax** v fax; ~ **un mensaje de texto** v text (send a message)

envolver v wrap

la época period (of time)

el equipaje luggage [baggage BE]; ~ **de mano** carry-on (piece of hand luggage)

el equipo team

el equipo equipment; ~ **de buceo** diving equipment; ~ **de esnórquel** snorkeling equipment

equis ele (XL) extra large

el error mistake

la erupción cutánea rash

las escaleras stairs; ~ **mecánicas** escalators

el escáner scanner

el escaparate window case

la escoba broom

el escozor sting

escribir v write; ~ **a máquina** v type

el escurridor colander

el esguince sprain

el esmalte enamel (jewelry)

eso that

la espalda back

España Spain

el español Spanish

la espátula spatula

la especialidad de la casa special (food)

el especialista specialist (doctor)

la espera n wait

esperar v wait

la espuma para el pelo mousse (hair)

el esquí n ski

esquiar v ski

los esquís acuáticos water skis

esta noche tonight

la estaca tent peg

la estación station; ~ **de autobuses** bus station; ~ **de metro** subway [underground BE] station; ~ **de tren** train [railway BE] station

el estadio stadium

el estado de

salud condition (medical)

los Estados Unidos United States (U.S.)

estadounidense American

el estanco tobacconist

el estanque pond

estar v be; ~ **de paso** v pass through

la estatua statue

el este east

el estilista hairstylist

esto this

el estómago stomach

estrellarse v crash (car)

estreñido constipated

estudiando studying

el estudiante student

estudiar v study

el euro euro

el exceso excess; ~ **de velocidad** speeding

la excursión excursion

experto expert (skill level)

la extensión extension (phone)

extraer v extract (tooth)

extraño strange

F

fácil adj easy

la factura bill (invoice BE)

la facturación check-in (airport)

facturar check (luggage)

la falda skirt

la familia family

la farmacia pharmacy [chemist BE]

el fax n fax

la fecha date (calendar)

feliz adj happy

feo adj ugly

el ferry ferry

la fianza deposit (to reserve a room)

la fiebre fever

el film transparente plastic wrap [cling film BE]

el fin de semana weekend

firmar v sign (name)

la flor flower

la fórmula infantil formula (baby)

el formulario form

la foto exposure (film); ~ photo; **~copia** photocopy; **~grafía** photography; ~ **digital** digital photo

la fregona mop

los frenos brakes (car)

frente a opposite

fresco fresh

frío adj cold (temperature)

las frutas y verduras produce

la frutería y verdulería produce store

el fuego fire

la fuente fountain

fuera outside

el fuerte fort

fumar v smoke

la funda para la cá-

mara camera case
el fútbol soccer [football BE]

G

las gafas glasses; ~ **de sol** sunglasses
el garaje garage (parking)
la garganta throat
la garrafa carafe
el gas butano cooking gas
la gasolina gas [petrol BE]; ~ **sin plomo** unleaded gas
la gasolinera gas [petrol BE] station
gay gay
el gerente manager
el gimnasio gym
el ginecólogo gynecologist
la gomina gel (hair)
la gota drop (medicine)
grabar v burn (CD); ~ v engrave
gracias thank you
los grados degrees (temperature); ~ **centígrado** Celsius
el gramo gram
grande large
los grandes almacenes department store
la granja farm
gratuito free
gris gray
la grúa tow truck
el grupo group
guapo attractive
guardar v save

(computer)
la guarnición side dish, order
el guía guide
la guía guide book; ~ **de tiendas** store directory
gustar v like; **me gusta** I like

H

ha sufrido daños damaged
la habitación room; ~ **individual** single room; ~ **libre** vacancy
hablar v speak
hacer v have; ~ **una apuesta** v place (a bet); ~ **un arreglo** v alter; ~ **una llamada** v phone; ~ **las maletas** v pack; ~ **turismo** sightseeing
hambriento hungry
helado icy
la hermana sister
el hermano brother
el hielo ice
el hígado liver (body part)
la hinchazón swelling
hipermétrope farsighted [long-sighted BE]
el hipódromo horsetrack
el hockey hockey; ~ **sobre hielo** ice hockey
la hoja de afeitar razor blade

hola hello
el hombre man
el hombro shoulder
hondo deeply
la hora hour
el horario n schedule [timetable BE]
los horarios hours; ~ **de atención al público** business hours; ~ **de oficina** office hours; ~ **de visita** visiting hours
las horas de consulta office hours (doctor's)
el hornillo camp stove
el horno stove
el hospital hospital
el hotel hotel
hoy today
el hueso bone

I

el ibuprofeno ibuprofen
la ida y vuelta round-trip [return BE]
la iglesia church
impresionante stunning
imprimir v print
el impuesto duty (tax)
incluir v include
inconsciente unconscious
increíble amazing
la infección vaginal vaginal infection
infectado infected
el inglés English
iniciar sesión v log on

(computer)
el insecto bug
la insolación sunstroke
el insomnio insomnia
la insulina insulin
interesante interesting
internacional international (airport area)
la internet internet
el/la intérprete interpreter
el intestino intestine
introducir v insert
ir a v go (somewhere)
ir de compras v go shopping
Irlanda Ireland
irlandés Irish
el IVA sales tax [VAT BE]
la izquierda left (direction)

J

el jabón soap
el jardín botánico botanical garden
el jazz jazz
el jersey sweater
joven young
las joyas jewelry
la joyería jeweler
jubilado retired
jugar v play
el juguete toy

K

el kilo kilo; ~**gramo** kilogram; ~**metraje** mileage
el kilómetro kilom-

eter; **~ cuadra-
do** square kilometer

L

el **labio** lip
la **laca** hairspray
el **ladrón** thief
el **lago** lake
la **lana** wool
la **lancha motora** motor boat
largo long
el **lavabo** sink
la **lavadora** washing machine
la **lavandería** laundromat [launderette BE]
lavar v wash
el **lavavajillas** dishwasher
la **lección** lesson
lejos far
la **lengua** tongue
la **lente** lens
las **lentillas de contacto** contact lens
las **letras** arts
las **libras esterlinas** pounds (British sterling)
libre de impuestos duty-free
la **librería** bookstore
el **libro** book
la **lima de uñas** nail file
limpiar v clean
la **limpieza de cutis** facial
limpio adj clean
la **línea** line (train)
el **lino** linen
la **linterna** flashlight

el **líquido** liquid; **~ de lentillas de contacto** lens solution; **~ lavavajillas** dishwashing liquid
listo ready
la **litera** berth
el **litro** liter
la **llamada** n call; **~ de teléfono** phone call; **~ despertador** wake-up call
llamar v call
la **llave** key; **~ de habitación** room key; **~ electrónica** key card
el **llavero** key ring
las **llegadas** arrivals (airport)
llegar v arrive
llenar v fill
llevar v take; **~ en coche** lift (to give a ride)
la **lluvia** rain
lluvioso rainy
lo siento sorry
localizar v reach
la **luz** light (overhead)

M

la **madre** mother
magnífico magnificent
el **malestar estomacal** upset stomach
la **maleta** bag, suitcase
la **mandíbula** jaw
las **mangas cortas** short sleeves
las **mangas lar-**

gas long sleeves
la **manicura** manicure
la **mano** hand
la **manta** blanket
mañana tomorrow; la **~** morning
el **mapa** ready; **~ de carreteras** road map; **~ de ciudad** town map; **~ de la pista** trail [piste BE] map
el **mar** sea
marcar v dial
mareado dizzy
el **mareo** motion [travel BE] sickness
el **marido** husband
marrón brown
el **martillo** hammer
más more; **~ alto** louder; **~ bajo** lower; **~ barato** cheaper; **~ despacio** slower; **~ grande** larger; **~ pequeño** smaller; **~ rápido** faster; **~ tarde** later; **~ temprano** earlier
el **masaje** massage; **~ deportivo** sports massage
el **mástil** tent pole
el **mecánico** mechanic
el **mechero** lighter
la **media hora** half hour
mediano medium (size)
la **medianoche** midnight
el **medicamento** medicine

el **médico** doctor
medio half; **~ kilo** half-kilo; **~día** noon [midday BE]
medir v measure (someone)
mejor best
menos less
el **mensaje** message; **~ instantáneo** instant message
el **mercado** market
el **mes** month
la **mesa** table
el **metro** subway [underground BE]
el **metro cuadrado** square meter
la **mezquita** mosque
el **microondas** microwave
el **minibar** mini-bar
el **minuto** minute
el **mirador** overlook [viewpoint BE] [scenic place]
mirar v look
la **misa** mass (church service)
mismo same
los **mocasines** loafers
la **mochila** backpack
molestar v bother
la **moneda** coin, currency
mono cute
la **montaña** n mountain
el **monumento conmemorativo** memorial (place)
morado purple

el mostrador de información information desk

mostrar v display

la moto acuática jet ski

la motocicleta motorcycle

movilidad mobility

la mujer wife, woman

la multa fine (fee for breaking law)

la muñeca doll; ~ wrist

el músculo muscle

el museo museum

la música music; ~ clásica classical music; ~ folk folk music; ~ pop pop music

el muslo thigh

N

nacional domestic

la nacionalidad nationality

nada nothing

nadar v swim

las nalgas buttocks

naranja orange (color)

la nariz nose

necesitar v need

los negocios business

negro black

nevado snowy

la nevera refrigerator

el nieto grandchild

la niña girl

el niño boy, child

el nivel intermedio intermediate

no no

la noche evening,

night

el nombre name; ~ de usuario username

normal regular

las normas de vestuario dress code

el norte north

la novia girlfriend

el novio boyfriend

el número number; ~ de fax fax number; ~ de permiso de conducir driver's license number; ~ de teléfono phone number; ~ de teléfono de información information (phone)

O

la obra de teatro n play (theater)

el oculista optician

el oeste west

la oficina office; ~ de correos post office; ~ de objetos perdidos lost and found; ~ de turismo tourist information office

el ojo eye

la olla pot

la ópera opera

el ordenador computer

la oreja ear

la orina urine

el oro gold; ~ amarillo yellow gold; ~ blanco white gold

la orquesta orchestra

oscuro dark

el otro camino alternate route

la oxígenoterapia oxygen treatment

P

padecer del corazón heart condition

el padre father

pagar v pay

el pájaro bird

el palacio palace; ~ de las cortes parliament building

los palillos chinos chopsticks

la panadería bakery

los pantalones pants [trousers BE]; ~ cortos shorts

el pañal diaper [nappy BE]

el pañuelo de paper tissue

el papel paper; ~ de aluminio aluminum [kitchen BE] foil; ~ de cocina paper towel; ~ higiénico toilet paper

el paquete package

para for; ~ llevar to go [take away BE]; ~ no fumadores non-smoking

el paracetamol acetaminophen [paracetamol BE]

la parada n stop; ~ de autobús bus stop

el paraguas umbrella

pararse v stop

el párking parking garage

el parque playpen; ~ park; ~ de atracciones amusement park

el partido game; ~ de fútbol soccer [football BE]; ~ de voleibol volleyball game

el pasajero passenger; ~ con billete ticketed passenger

el pasaporte passport

el pase de acceso a los remontes lift pass

el pasillo aisle

la pasta de dientes toothpaste

la pastelería pastry shop

el patio de recreo playground

el peatón pedestrian

el pecho chest (body part)

el pediatra pediatrician

la pedicura pedicure

pedir v order

el peinado hairstyle

el peine comb

la película movie

peligroso dangerous

el pelo hair

el peltre pewter

la peluquería de caballeros barber

la peluquería hair salon

los pendientes earrings

el pene penis

la penicilina penicillin

la pensión bed and breakfast

pequeño small

perder v lose (something)

perdido lost

el perfume perfume

el periódico newspaper

la perla pearl

permitir v allow, permit

el perro guía guide dog

la persona con discapacidad visual visually impaired person

la picadura de insecto insect bite

picante spicy

picar v stamp (a ticket)

el pie foot

la piel skin

la pierna leg

la pieza part (for car)

los pijamas pajamas

la pila battery

la píldora Pill (birth control)

la piscina pool; ~ **cubierta** indoor pool; ~ **exterior** outdoor pool; ~ **infantil** kiddie [paddling BE] pool

la pista trail [piste BE]

la pizzería pizzeria

el placer pleasure

la plancha n iron (clothes)

planchar v iron

la planta floor [storey BE]; ~ **baja** ground floor

la plata silver; ~ **esterlina** sterling silver

el platino platinum

el plato dish (kitchen); ~ **principal** main course

la playa beach

la plaza town square

la policía police

la pomada cream (ointment)

ponerse en contacto con v contact

por for; ~ per; ~ **día** per day; ~ **favor** please; ~ **hora** per hour; ~ **la noche** overnight; ~ **noche** per night; ~ **semana** per week

el postre dessert

el precio price

precioso beautiful

el prefijo area code

la pregunta question

presentar v introduce

el preservativo condom

la primera clase first class

primero first

los principales sitios de interés main attraction

principiante beginner,

novice (skill level)

la prioridad de paso right of way

la prisa rush

el probador fitting room

probar v taste

el problema problem

el producto good; ~ **de limpieza** cleaning product

programar v schedule

prohibir v prohibit

el pronóstico forecast

pronunciar v pronounce

el protector solar sunscreen

provisional temporary

próximo next

el público public

el pueblo village

el puente bridge

la puerta gate (airport); ~ door; ~ **de incendios** fire door

el pulmón lung

la pulsera bracelet

el puro cigar

Q

qué what (question)

quedar bien v fit (clothing)

quedarse v stay

la queja complaint

la quemadura solar sunburn

querer v love (someone)

quién who (question)

el quiosco newsstand

R

la ración portion; ~ **para niños** children's portion

la rampa para silla de ruedas wheelchair ramp

el rap rap (music)

rápido express, fast

la raqueta racket (sports); ~ **de nieve** snowshoe

la reacción alérgica allergic reaction

recargar v recharge

la recepción reception

la receta prescription

recetar v prescribe

rechazar v decline (credit card)

recibir v receive

el recibo receipt

reciclar recycling

recoger v pick up (something)

la recogida de equipajes baggage claim

la recomendación recommendation

recomendar v recommend

el recorrido tour; ~ **en autobús** bus tour; ~ **turístico** sightseeing tour

recto straight

el recuerdo souvenir

el regalo gift

la región region

el registro check-in (hotel); ~ **del coche** vehicle registration

la regla period (menstrual)

el Reino Unido United Kingdom (U.K.)

la relación relationship

rellenar v fill out (form)

el reloj watch; **~ de pared** wall clock

el remolque trailer

reparar v fix (repair)

el repelente de insectos insect repellent

repetir v repeat

la resaca hangover

la reserva reservation; **~ natural** nature preserve

reservar v reserve

el/la residente de la UE EU resident

respirar v breathe

el restaurante restaurant

retirar v withdraw; **~ fondos** withdrawal (bank)

retrasarse v delay

la reunión meeting

revelar v develop (film)

revisar v check (on something)

la revista magazine

el riñón kidney (body part)

el río river

robado stolen

robar v steal

el robo theft

la rodilla knee

rojo red

romántico romantic

romper v break

la ropa clothing; **~ interior** underwear

rosa pink

roto broken

el rugby rugby

la rueda tire (tyre BE); **~ pinchada** flat tire (tyre BE)

las ruinas ruins

la ruta route; **~ de senderismo** walking route

S

la sábana sheet

el sacacorchos corkscrew

el saco de dormir sleeping bag

la sala room; **~ de conciertos** concert hall; **~ de espera** waiting room; **~ de reuniones** meeting room

la salida check-out (hotel)

la salida n exit; **~ de urgencia** emergency exit

las salidas departures (airport)

salir v exit, leave

el salón room; **~ de congresos** convention hall; **~ de juegos recreativos** arcade; **~ de manicura** nail salon

¡Salud! Cheers!

la salud health

las sandalias sandals

sangrar v bleed

la sangre blood

el santuario shrine

la sartén frying pan

la sauna sauna

el secador de pelo hair dryer

la secreción discharge (bodily fluid)

la seda silk

sediento thirsty

la seguridad security

el seguro insurance

seguro safe (protected)

el sello n stamp (postage)

el semáforo traffic light

la semana week

semanal weekly

el seminario seminar

el sendero trail; **~ para bicicletas** bike route

el seno breast

sentarse v sit

separado separated (marriage)

ser v be

serio serious

el servicio restroom (toilet BE); **~ service** (in a restaurant); **~ completo** full-service; **~ de habitaciones** room service; **~ inalámbrico a internet** wireless internet service; **~ de internet** internet service; **~ de lavandería** laundry service; **~ de limpieza de habitaciones** housekeeping service

la servilleta napkin

sí yes

el sida AIDS

la silla chair; **~ para niños** child seat; **~ de ruedas** wheelchair

el símbolo symbol (keyboard)

sin without; **~ alcohol** non-alcoholic; **~ grasa** fat free; **~ receta** over the counter (medication)

la sinagoga synagogue

el sitio de interés attraction (place)

el sobre envelope

el socorrista lifeguard

el sol sun

solamente only

soleado sunny

solo alone

soltero single (marriage)

el sombrero hat

la somnolencia drowsiness

sordo deaf

soso bland

el suavizante conditioner

el subtítulo subtitle

sucio dirty

la sudadera sweatshirt

el suelo floor

el sujetador bra

súper super (fuel)

superior upper
el supermercado grocery store, supermarket
la supervisión supervision
el sur south
el surfista windsurfer

T

la tabla board; ~ **de snowboard** snowboard; ~ **de surf** surfboard
la talla size; ~ **grande** plus size; ~ **pequeña** petite size
el taller garage (repair)
el talón de equipaje luggage [baggage BE] ticket
el tampón tampon
la taquilla locker; reservation desk
tarde late (time)
la tarde afternoon
la tarjeta card; ~ **de cajero automático** ATM card; ~ **de crédito** credit card; ~ **de débito** debit card; ~ **de embarque** boarding pass; ~ **internacional de estudiante** international student card; ~ **de memoria** memory card; ~ **de negocios** business card; ~ **postal** postcard; ~ **de seguro** insurance card; ~ **de socio** membership card; ~ **telefónica** phone card
la tasa fee
el taxi taxi
la taza cup; ~ **medidora** measuring cup
el teatro theater; ~ **de la ópera** opera house
la tela impermeable groundcloth [groundsheet BE]
el teleférico cable car
el teléfono telephone; ~ **móvil** cell [mobile BE] phone; ~ **público** pay phone
la telesilla chair lift
el telesquí ski/drag lift
la televisión TV
el templo temple (religious)
temprano early
el tenedor fork
tener v have; ~ **dolor** v hurt (have pain); ~ **náuseas** v be nauseous
el tenis tennis
la tensión arterial blood pressure
la terminal terminal (airport)
terminar v end
la terracotta terracotta
terrible terrible
el texto n text (message)
el tiempo time; ~ **weather**
la tienda store; ~ **de alimentos naturales** health food store; ~ **de antigüedades** antique store; ~ **de bebidas alcohólicas** liquor store [off-licence BE]; ~ **de campaña** tent; ~ **de deportes** sporting goods store; ~ **de fotografía** camera store; ~ **de juguetes** toy store; ~ **de música** music store; ~ **de recuerdos** souvenir store; ~ **de regalos** gift shop; ~ **de ropa** clothing store
las tijeras scissors
la tintorería dry cleaner
el tipo de cambio exchange rate
tirar v pull (door sign)
la tirita bandage
la toalla towel
la toallita baby wipe
el tobillo ankle
el torneo de golf golf tournament
la torre tower
la tos n cough
toser v cough
el total total (amount)
trabajar v work
tradicional traditional
traducir v translate
traer v bring

tragar v swallow
el traje suit
tranquilo quiet
el tren train; ~ **rápido** express train
triste sad
la trona highchair
el trozo piece
la tumbona deck chair
el turista tourist

U

último last
la universidad university
uno one
la uña nail; ~ **del dedo** fingernail; ~ **del pie** toenail
urgente urgent
usar v use

V

las vacaciones vacation [holiday BE]
vaciar v empty
la vacuna vaccination
la vagina vagina
la validez valid
valioso valuable
el valle valley
el valor value
el vaquero denim
los vaqueros jeans
el vaso glass (drinking)
el váter químico chemical toilet
vegetariano vegetarian
la vejiga bladder
vender v sell
el veneno poison

venir v come
la ventana window
el ventilador fan (appliance)
ver v see
verde green
el vestido dress (piece of clothing)
el viaje trip
el vidrio glass (material)

viejo old
la viña vineyard
la violación n rape
violar v rape
el visado visa (passport document)
visitar v visit
la vitamina vitamin
la vitrina display case
viudo widowed
vivir v live

vomitar v vomit
el vuelo flight; ~ **internacional** international flight; ~ **nacional** domestic flight

Z

la zapatería shoe store
las zapatillas slippers; ~ **de deporte** sneaker
los zapatos shoes
la zona area; ~ **de compras** shopping area; ~ **de fumadores** smoking area; ~ **para picnic** picnic area
el zoológico zoo
zurcir v mend

INDEX

Berlitz pocket guide

BARCELONA

Sixteenth Edition 2019

Editor: Tatiana Wilde
Author: Neil Schlecht
Head of DTP and Pre-Press: Rebeka Davies
Managing Editor: Carine Tracanelli
Picture Editor: Tom Smyth
Cartography Update: Carte
Update Production: Apa Digital
Photography Credits: Alamy 101; AWL Images
1; Corbis 17; Corrie Wingate/Apa Publications
4ML, 4TL, 5TC, 5MC, 5M, 5MC, 5M, 6L, 7, 13,
14, 27, 29, 30, 31, 32, 34, 37, 38, 43, 47, 48, 50,
57, 59, 61, 63, 64, 65, 66, 68, 71, 74, 78, 87, 97;
Dreamstime.com 80; Getty Images 4MC, 24,
53, 91, 98; Greg Gladman/Apa Publications
7R, 18, 72, 82, 85, 89, 102; Gregory Wrona/
Apa Publications 41; iStock 4TC, 11, 55, 77,
94; Public domain 20; Ronald Stallard/Museu
Picasso 5T, 45; Shutterstock 6R, 93
Cover Picture: Luigi Vaccarella/4Corners

Distribution
UK, Ireland and Europe: Apa Publications
(UK) Ltd; sales@insightguides.com
United States and Canada: Ingram
Publisher Services; ips@ingramcontent.com
Australia and New Zealand: Woodslane;
info@woodslane.com.au
Southeast Asia: Apa Publications (SN) Pte;
singaporeoffice@insightguides.com
Worldwide: Apa Publications (UK) Ltd;
sales@insightguides.com

**Special Sales, Content Licensing
and CoPublishing**
Insight Guides can be purchased in bulk
quantities at discounted prices. We can
create special editions, personalised jackets
and corporate imprints tailored to your
needs. sales@insightguides.com;
www.insightguides.biz

Contact us
Every effort has been made to provide
accurate information in this publication,
but changes are inevitable. The publisher
cannot be responsible for any resulting loss,
inconvenience or injury. We would appreciate
it if readers would call our attention to any
errors or outdated information. We also
welcome your suggestions; please contact
us at: berlitz@apaguide.co.uk
www.insightguides.com/berlitz

Barcelona Transport

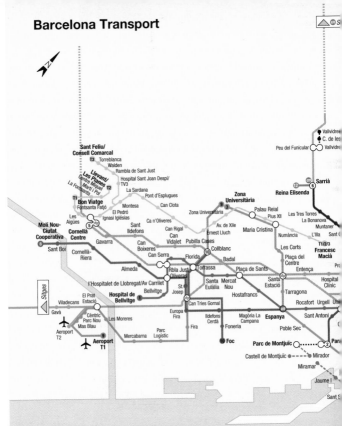

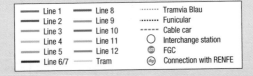

▬▬▬ Line 1	▬▬▬ Line 8	········ Tramvia Blau	
▬▬▬ Line 2	▬▬▬ Line 9	········ Funicular	
▬▬▬ Line 3	▬▬▬ Line 10	········ Cable car	
▬▬▬ Line 4	▬▬▬ Line 11	○ Interchange station	
▬▬▬ Line 5	▬▬▬ Line 12	Ⓕ FGC	
▬▬▬ Line 6/7	▬▬▬ Tram	Ⓡ Connection with RENFE	

C000254646

THE LITTLE
BOOK FOR
YOGA
LOVERS

JO PETERS

An Hachette UK Company
www.hachette.co.uk

Vie Books, an imprint of Summersdale Publishers
Part of Octopus Publishing Group Limited
Carmelite House
50 Victoria Embankment
LONDON
EC4Y 0DZ
UK

www.summersdale.com

Printed and bound in China

ISBN: 978-1-83799-410-6

Substantial discounts on bulk quantities of Summersdale books are available to corporations, professional associations and other organizations. For details contact general enquiries: telephone: +44 (0) 1243 771107 or email: enquiries@summersdale.com.

Disclaimer
Neither the author nor the publisher can be held responsible for any injury, loss or claim – be it health, financial or otherwise – arising out of the use, or misuse, of the suggestions made herein. Always consult your doctor before trying any new form of exercise if you have a medical or health condition, or are worried about any of the side effects. This book is not intended as a substitute for the medical advice of a doctor or physician.

CONTENTS

INTRODUCTION

Welcome to this book bursting with tips, tricks, lessons and learnings to help you fall even further in love with the wonderful world of yoga.

You may be a practised yogi wishing to elevate your life beyond the mat, you may be a beginner craving a deeper understanding of the practical techniques, or you may never have attempted yoga at all but have glimpsed the radiant glow of those who have and are wondering how they achieve it. Wherever you are on your yoga journey, this book will enlighten your mind and inspire your practice.

Yoga is a holistic activity that enriches the mind, body and soul. It can be adapted to your different needs, supporting you at your lowest ebb and boosting you at your highest. It is a practice for absolutely everyone, and there are many different reasons why one may fall in love with it.

Many sports have the added advantages of boosting mood and clearing the mind, but yoga is unique in having that as its central purpose. Yoga is inherently entwined with meditation and is designed to leave you feeling peaceful and content.

Physically, yoga stretches, flexes and strengthens the body. It is often prescribed as rehabilitative exercise for its multitude of physical benefits. There are many different styles of yoga, from the restorative to the powerful, so everybody can experience it in a way that feels right to them and reap the rewards they desire.

Yoga also extends far beyond personal practice. It brings together whole communities to cultivate supportive spaces in which everyone can feel safe and cared for. Unlike other exercise classes, yoga has an ancient history based in spirituality and moral codes that focus on bettering not just your own existence but the existence of everyone around you too.

Throughout these pages, we will explore many of the facets that make up the whole system and learn how yoga is not merely movement on the mat but an entire way of life. We will consider the historic roots that yoga has grown from and how it has branched out, and we will break down the alignment of some fundamental postures into their distinctive elements. Throughout the book, you'll be learning common yogic vocabulary and etiquette to ensure you're ready to step into any classroom. You will go on to develop the basics to elevate your practice on and off the mat and allow your love for yoga to blossom into a way of living that brings you tranquillity and gratitude.

THE
FUNDAMENTALS
OF YOGA

As any yoga lover knows, it is easy to fall in love with yoga having only experienced it as a set of physical movements, mindful breathwork and a meditative guide. But yoga extends far beyond that.

In order to deepen your practice and strengthen your connection to it, both on and off the mat, it is important to learn and appreciate the fundamentals of yoga and what it means to live a yogic life.

This chapter will introduce the physical practice of yoga and explain where it originated and how it is enjoyed across all corners of the world today. It will provide an overview of the different types of yoga and break down into their separate components many of the key elements that can be found in any given yoga class.

It will also start to demystify some of the terminology and traditions to ensure you turn up to class with a better understanding and appreciation for the ancient art.

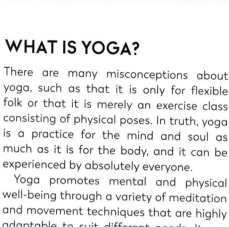

WHAT IS YOGA?

There are many misconceptions about yoga, such as that it is only for flexible folk or that it is merely an exercise class consisting of physical poses. In truth, yoga is a practice for the mind and soul as much as it is for the body, and it can be experienced by absolutely everyone.

Yoga promotes mental and physical well-being through a variety of meditation and movement techniques that are highly adaptable to suit different needs. It can range from absolute stillness to powerful strength exercises, from deep relaxation to focused meditation.

What originated as a spiritual philosophy has evolved to offer a whole host of benefits to those who practise it. It can help you lead a more calm, grateful and mindful life way beyond the duration of a yoga class.

THE HISTORY OF YOGA

Yoga began in northern India. While its exact origins are unknown, it is referenced in sacred texts from over 5,000 years ago and has a rich history that is entwined with Buddhism and Hinduism.

The word "yoga" is derived from the Sanskrit word *yuj*, which means "to join" or "to unite", in reference to the yogic purpose of bringing together body and mind as well as uniting the individual's consciousness with the universe. A core tenet of yogic philosophy is recognizing that we are all part of one whole.

Yoga started as a meditative practice and has been developed to incorporate the body and the postures (or asanas).

A key contributor to this evolution was an Indian sage named Patanjali, who wrote Sanskrit texts called the *Yoga Sutras* that began to break down yoga into different "limbs" and to explore how it could be practised both physically and in everyday life.

*Here and now is
where yoga begins.*

LIMBS OF YOGA

Patanjali's *Yoga Sutras* outline eight limbs to help you practise with greater purpose and live a more meditative, meaningful life.

1   **YAMA:** Guidance on how we interact with the world around us, including truthfulness, non-violence and selflessness.

2   **NIYAMA:** More personal focuses, such as cleanliness, contentment and spirituality.

3   **ASANA:** Within the *Yoga Sutras*, the Sanskrit word "asana" refers to the posture for meditation, but we now use it to describe the physical postures of yoga.

4   **PRANAYAMA:** Breathing techniques that can deepen, free and control the breath.

5   **PRATYAHARA:** Meaning "sense withdrawal", this limb focuses on withdrawing from the distractions around us.

6   **DHARANA:** Without distractions, *dharana* is where we put our focus through meditative techniques that increase concentration.

7   **DHYANA:** The act of truly meditating.

8   **SAMADHI:** The "bliss" or "enlightenment" achieved through all the other limbs.

YOGA STYLE: HATHA

Many branches of yoga are taught around the world, so let us explore a few of the most popular styles, beginning with Hatha, one of the most traditional physical practices.

A Hatha yoga class will feature a selection of postures and breathing techniques that aim to unify the mind, body and spirit.

Hatha yoga is usually a more accessible style for beginners, with static postures that are held for around five breaths and the practitioner often resetting in a neutral pose before the next one.

The Sanskrit term *ha* means "sun" and *ta* means "moon", and Hatha emphasizes the need for balance and equilibrium. Many asanas will be followed by another that counteracts the first; for example, a backbend followed by a forward fold.

Hatha yoga is often a great place to start out on a yoga journey, as it presents an opportunity to learn many of the fundamental asanas that are used throughout other styles.

YOGA STYLE: VINYASA

Vinyasa is a flowing style of yoga that consists of a fluid movement between postures and a focus on moving with the breath.

The word "Vinyasa" comes from the Sanskrit and means "to move (or place) in a special way", highlighting the style's concern with entering and exiting asanas, as well as the asanas themselves.

Vinyasa classes, sometimes called Flow classes, will often start slowly to allow you a chance to connect with your breath, before moving through a curated sequence of postures. Sections of the sequence might be repeated to help you sink into a meditative flow. There is emphasis on the rhythm of inhaling and exhaling and allowing that to dictate the pace.

Instructors of Vinyasa will often cue interesting transitions between asanas, and classes consist of more continuous movement than Hatha yoga. Vinyasa can be tailored to beginners and advanced yogis. Be sure to choose a class suitable for you.

INHALE WHAT SERVES YOU, EXHALE WHAT DOESN'T

YOGA STYLE: ASHTANGA

Ashtanga is a powerful yoga style featuring a set sequence of asanas and dynamic Vinyasa flows.

Ashtanga yoga has beginner, intermediate and advanced sequences, but all begin with five rounds of Sun Salutations (Surya Namaskara A and B) and close with Savasana (Corpse Pose).

Traditionally, Ashtanga is taught in "Mysore style" (named after the Indian city in which it originated), where there is no instructor leading the class and participants flow through the learned sequence to the pace of their own breath. Teachers are there to make adjustments and help improve asana alignment.

Ashtanga has given rise to many forms of power yoga, which focus heavily on strength-based postures and fast-paced flows. If you're new to Ashtanga, it's important to check the class will be suitable for beginners, with cues and modifications, as it is generally quite an intense practice.

YOGA STYLE: YIN

Yin is an incredibly meditative form of yoga, where the practice is slowed right down. Each pose is held for 3–5 minutes to allow the mind to sink into deeper meditation and the body to unwind.

Holding the asanas for longer enables you to stretch beyond the muscles and release tension from the body's fascia, the interconnecting tissue between muscles. Props are often used within Yin classes, such as bolsters and cushions to help you find stillness for longer.

Despite the slow pace, Yin classes can often be incredibly challenging in a different way to Vinyasa and Ashtanga. Maintaining physical and mental stillness requires discipline. Without constant cues and movements, the mind tends to wander off and the body wants to fidget.

Yin is not only deeply relaxing but also a great way to increase mindfulness and flexibility.

Yoga is a metaphor for life.
You have to take it really slowly.
You can't rush.
You can't skip to the
next position.

MADONNA

YOGA STYLE: IYENGAR

Named after its originator, Iyengar yoga focuses on finding the perfect alignment within physical postures in order to feel balanced within the mind and body, with asanas ranging from simple to complex.

Iyengar yoga often uses many props, including blocks, bolsters, straps, chairs and walls, to help everyone achieve precise alignment despite any injuries or muscle tightness. Since it recognizes that all bodies are different, Iyengar yoga can be a great practice if the pace or intensity of other styles doesn't work for you. Iyengar ensures everyone can practise safely.

It is also a great way for experienced yoga students to ensure they are finding the correct alignment in asanas, which can sometimes be forgotten about in faster-paced classes. Holding the postures for longer than a Vinyasa class, for example, helps build mobility, stability and strength.

BENEFITS OF YOGA

That yoga has lived on for thousands of years is testimony to the ways in which people have consistently found solace and positivity in the practice.

Thanks to the many different branches of yoga that have evolved, there is a yoga style to suit every need and provide an abundance of benefits, including:

- Increased flexibility and mobility
- Strengthened muscles, including core, arms, back and legs
- Improved balance
- Deeper and more efficient breathing
- Improved sleep quality
- Greater clarity and clear-headedness
- A more profound peacefulness
- Deeper relaxation
- A greater sense of gratitude
- A deeper connection with your body
- Boosted self-confidence

You may feel different benefits each time you practise, depending on what you are bringing to the mat that day. Often the benefits travel way beyond the classroom and can help you find peace and contentment in day-to-day life.

WAYS TO PRACTISE

Yoga should be practised wherever you feel most comfortable and wherever suits your financial and accessibility needs best.

Classes

In a classroom, you have a qualified teacher there to ensure you're in the correct alignment and to help you into trickier postures. Being in a classroom also gives you a chance to meet your local yoga community.

At home

Practising at home can help you better your confidence and avoid comparing yourself to others. It can be easier to fit into your schedule, and not much space or equipment is required. However, you should not attempt postures that you're not confident in without professional supervision.

Retreats

Retreats offer the opportunity for you to become more deeply connected to your practice and to build up at a slower pace. They enable you a greater chance of meditation by taking a prolonged step away from your usual schedule.

YOGA EQUIPMENT

Yoga doesn't require any special equipment at all. You can fulfil the yogic mindset without even a mat! However, there are props available to help with alignment and comfort.

- **MAT:** The thicker the mat, the more cushioning it offers, but the harder it is for balancing poses.
- **BLOCK:** Blocks can be held or sat on to access asanas. Substitute at home with a thick book.
- **BOLSTER:** A tubular cushion to soften postures. Substitute with a cushion or rolled-up towel.
- **STRAP:** A length of material used to extend your reach. Substitute with a belt or a dressing gown cord.
- **BLANKET:** Used for gentle cushioning or staying warm in meditative stillness.

Wear clothes that allow you to move freely, and bare feet is recommended for grip. Wearing layers is advisable to control body temperature.

ESSENTIAL
YOGA POSES

Asanas make up the bulk of most contemporary yoga classes. It's through these physical poses that yoga helps to increase your flexibility, strength and stability.

Different asanas target different areas of the body through stretching, twisting, lengthening, holding and balancing. Often one pose challenges multiple body parts at once!

Each pose should be held in the correct alignment to prevent injury and allow you to reap the benefits. There are a multitude of ways to safely modify asanas by scaling them up or down in intensity. Even for experienced yogis, the same asana can feel harder or easier on different days. It is crucial to listen to your body.

This chapter will explore a few fundamental beginner, intermediate and advanced yoga poses, outlining their purpose, key alignment details and points of focus.

Unless otherwise specified, try holding these postures for five steady breaths on a yoga mat.

EASY POSE (SUKHASANA)

Beginner

Asana literally means "seat", and it is important to master a comfortable, correctly aligned seated position before all else. Many yoga teachers will spend some time dedicated solely to breathing and meditation in a posture such as Sukhasana.

1   Come to a gentle cross-legged position, allowing your hips to open. If this hurts your knees, reduce their angles by placing one foot slightly in front of the other.

2   Lift the crown of your head up towards the ceiling, elongating your spine. This should create space around your ribcage and diaphragm.

3   Place the backs of your hands against your knees, palms facing up. Drop your shoulders away from your ears, releasing any held tension.

You can modify this posture by sitting on a block to elevate your hips or in a chair with both feet on the floor.

CHILD'S POSE (BALASANA)
Beginner

Child's Pose is a restorative pose that gently opens the hips, releases tension from the spine and allows you to focus on breathing. Return to this pose whenever you need to feel grounded.

1   Place your knees as wide as the mat's edge and bring your toes together behind you. If this is uncomfortable, bring your knees together and keep your thighs parallel.

2   Send your hips back towards your heels, pressing your sitting bones down towards the mat.

3   Place your arms in front of you, outstretched but relaxed.

4   Rest your forehead on the mat or on a block or cushion for a gentler stretch.

5   As you inhale, feel your ribcage expanding into your back.

6   As you exhale, imagine yourself sinking further into the mat. Try to relax through your head, chest, hips and sitting bones.

CAT-COW (MARJARYASANA-BITILASANA)

Beginner

Cat-Cow brings gentle movement into the back, opens the chest and helps you to tune into the rhythm of your breath.

1   Find a tabletop position on your hands and knees. Make sure your wrists are aligned with your shoulders and your knees are aligned with your hips.

2   As you exhale, press your palms and knees into the mat and lift your navel up, creating a curve in your back. Think about pushing the ground away from you. This is "cat".

3   As you inhale, drop your belly back down and lift the crown of your head and your tailbone up towards the sky, creating an arch through your back. Think about opening your chest out. This is "cow".

4   Flow between cat and cow to the rhythm of your breath, feeling your spine loosening up.

DOWNWARD-FACING DOG (ADHO MUKHA SVANASANA)

Beginner

Downward-Facing Dog is synonymous with yoga. It stretches the back, strengthens the upper body and is one of the gentler inversions (where the hips are above the head). Alignment is key here and worth taking time to perfect.

1   From a tabletop position, lift your hips up and begin to straighten through your legs and spine. Imagine you are creating a triangle, with your tailbone forming the top point. As you learn this pose, you can leave a gentle bend in your knees.

2   Ensure your hands are shoulder-width apart with your fingers gently spread, pressing down.

3   Feet should be hip-width apart. Aim to keep your heels on the mat, although this might not be possible until your hamstrings are more flexible.

4   Gaze towards your navel so that your neck continues the straight line of your spine.

COBRA (BHUJANGASANA)
Beginner

Cobra is a gentle backbend used in traditional Sun Salutations. This pose can be modified to be gentler, to Sphinx Pose, or harder, to Upward-Facing Dog.

1   Lie on your stomach with your hands directly beneath your shoulders. Press through your palms, straightening through your arms and lifting your chest away from the mat.

2   Keep your legs parallel, extending out behind you, with the soles of your feet facing upwards.

3   Imagine your head pulling up to the sky and your chest opening. Keep your shoulders relaxed, pulling softly downwards.

4   You can gently engage your buttocks if that feels more protective of your spine, or release them completely, breathing into your lower back to create space.

5   If it's comfortable, you can gaze upwards, gently tipping your head back to increase the stretch in your neck.

MOUNTAIN POSE (TADASANA)
Beginner

Mountain Pose is about finding the balance between neutrality and engagement and is often used to recentre between postures. Tadasana may also be referred to as Samasthiti, meaning "equal standing".

1   Stand at the top of your mat, big toes together and heels slightly apart. Feel all four corners of your feet grounded into the mat. Allow your arms to gently rest by your side.

2   Lift the crown of your head up towards the sky while relaxing your shoulders downwards. Feel the full length of your spine and the space around your ribcage to take full breaths.

3   Focus on activating your core. Although it is a neutral posture, it is not total relaxation. You should feel engaged and stable.

4   Close your eyes or soften your gaze on a point in front of you.

SEATED TWIST (ARDHA MATSYENDRASANA)

Beginner

Twists wring out the core body, releasing tension in the abdomen and back. This posture is the most accessible twist. It may also be referred to as Half Lord of the Fishes Pose.

1   Sit with both legs outstretched. Bend your right leg and place your right foot on the outside of your left knee. Your left leg can remain straight or you can tuck it in.

2   Place the fingertips of your right hand behind you for support. As you inhale, extend your left arm up.

3   As you exhale, twist towards your right leg, hugging your knee with your left arm. You can take the twist further by hooking your left elbow to the outside of your right knee.

4   As you inhale, focus on lengthening your spine. As you exhale, twist deeper.

5   Repeat on the other side.

CORPSE POSE (SAVASANA)

Beginner

Many yoga classes end with some time spent in Savasana to unwind and meditate. As the name suggests, Corpse Pose is the only yoga pose that requires no muscular engagement and is one of total relaxation.

1   Lie on your back and gently close your eyes.

2   With your legs outstretched, allow your ankles to roll out to the sides. You can place a bolster beneath your knees for comfort.

3   Keep your arms outstretched with your palms facing upwards.

4   Relax your shoulders and your jaw. Allow your belly to gently rise and fall with your breath.

5   Ensure every part of you is free from tension. Allow yourself to be heavy and sink into the mat.

6   You can place something soft behind your head and cover yourself with a blanket for warmth – whatever enables you to find stillness and peace in this posture.

7   Stay here for 5–10 minutes.

WARRIOR 1 (VIRABHADRASANA I)

Intermediate

Warrior poses are included in most Sun Salutations. They strengthen and stretch the lower body. If you hold the posture correctly, for five breaths, you will start to feel the fire of your thigh muscles!

1   From a position of feet together, take a deep step back with your left leg.

2   Make a 90-degree bend in your right leg. Ensure your knee is directly over your ankle.

3   Keep your back leg straight. Your left foot should be at a 45-degree angle, toes facing outwards, with your heel grounded. If this is uncomfortable, lift your heel and face your foot forwards instead (this is High Lunge Pose).

4   Inhale and lift your arms above your head, keeping them shoulder-width apart, with your palms facing each other.

5   Stay strong and focus your energy forwards, feeling a stretch in your hips.

6   Repeat on the other side.

WARRIOR 2 (VIRABHADRASANA II)

Intermediate

Warrior 2 involves your hip and chest opening and is a strengthening challenge on your arms. It is easier to transition from Warrior 1 to 2 than the other way around because of the angle of the back foot.

1 From Warrior 1 Pose, keep the exact same position of your front leg (bend in the knee, right foot facing forwards), but turn your back foot to fully face the long edge of the mat, planting your heel down. Keep your back leg straight.

2 Turn your torso to the long edge, opening through your chest.

3 Let your arms come to shoulder height, parallel to the floor.

4 Gaze at the middle finger on your front hand so your head is facing the front of your mat.

5 Keep your chest directly above your hips and both arms engaged.

6 Repeat on the other side.

TRIANGLE POSE (TRIKONASANA)

Intermediate

Triangle Pose gets even deeper into the hip space and challenges your full-body awareness (proprioception).

1   Take a long step back with your left leg and place your foot at a 90-degree angle. Your right foot remains facing forwards. Keep both legs straight.

2   As you inhale, lift your arms to shoulder height.

3   As you exhale, send your right arm forwards, pulling your body over your front leg. Once you can stretch no further forwards, bring the fingertips of your right hand down to the inside of your right ankle, to the mat or to a block. Your left hand reaches up to the sky.

4   If it's not uncomfortable, gaze up at your left hand.

5   Repeat on the other side.

A tip is to imagine you are between two walls; you want all your body on one vertical line.

PIGEON (MODIFICATION OF EKA PADA RAJAKAPOTASANA)

Intermediate

Pigeon posture is a deep hip-opener. Tight hips can inhibit emotional openness, so often postures like Pigeon can feel emotionally invigorating, too.

1   From a plank position, bring your right knee forwards, behind your right wrist, and place it on the mat. Place your right foot behind your left wrist. Your shin doesn't need to be parallel with the mat's front edge if that's uncomfortable on your knee – you can bring your right foot further back.

2   Send your left toes backwards and lower your hips to the mat, keeping them even. If one hip dips lower, place a blanket or block underneath it.

3   You can stay with your torso upright or walk your hands forwards and lower your chest down.

4   Every time you exhale, allow your hips to sink further towards the mat.

5   Repeat on the other side.

TREE POSE (VRKSASANA)

Intermediate

Tree Pose helps build your confidence with balancing and can improve your posture, hip mobility and lower body strength. To make it easier, use a wall for balance; to make it harder, close your eyes!

1   Ground your left foot into the mat and lift your right.

2   Place the sole of your right foot on the inside of your left leg, anywhere from calf to inner thigh. To avoid injury, do not place your foot in line with your left knee. Keep your right knee perpendicular to your body to open up your hips.

3   Bring your hands to a prayer position or above your head and focus on a fixed point in front of you.

4   Try to find length in your spine and stability in your grounded leg.

5   Repeat on the other side.

WARRIOR 3 (VIRABHADRASANA III)

Intermediate

Warrior 3 is a balancing posture that requires strength in the core and buttocks, as well as flexibility in the hamstrings and good proprioception.

1   Start in a lunge and transfer your weight forwards until you are fully weighted on the front foot and can pick your back foot off the mat.

2   Keep your lifted leg straight, your foot flexed and your chest forwards. Aim to make a T-shape. Imagine a horizontal line running from your back heel to the back of your head – although this may take time to perfect.

3   Hold your hands in a prayer position or out in front of you. You can keep a small bend in the grounded leg if that makes you feel more stable.

4   Repeat on the other side.

The most important part of balancing poses is to have fun!

BRIDGE POSE
(SETU BANDHA SARVANGASANA)
Intermediate

Bridge Pose is a backbend that stretches the front body and strengthens the back. A power yoga class might feature a dynamic Bridge Pose to work out the glutes, while a Yin class may use it restoratively, with the body supported by blocks.

1   Lying on your back, bend your knees and place the soles of your feet in line with your sitting bones. You should be able to just about brush your ankles with your fingertips.

2   Focus on pressing your feet into the mat. Feel this energetic pull firing up your ankles, calves, thighs and buttocks.

3   Once your legs are engaged, lift your tailbone away from the mat, raising your hips upwards.

4   Keep your knees parallel to your hips and your neck relaxed but straight.

SHOULDER STAND (SALAMBA SARVANGASANA)

Intermediate

Shoulder Stand is an inversion that can help to reduce fatigue and improve digestion. But it is vital to learn the correct alignment and practise carefully, using as much support as needed.

1   Lie on your back with your arms by your sides, gently pressing down.

2   As you inhale, lift your legs up and over your head (this may need some controlled momentum). Allow your lower back to peel off the mat so that you're weighted on your upper back and shoulders.

3   Bend your elbows and place your hands either side of your spine for support.

4   Stretch your legs upwards, pointing your toes. Aim to get your toes, legs and hips as directly over your shoulders as possible.

5   Gaze at your navel, keeping your neck straight.

6   Hold for ten breaths, if comfortable.

LOTUS POSE (PADMASANA)
Advanced

Lotus Pose requires very mobile hips and knees. Some highly experienced yogis will never achieve Lotus because it doesn't suit their anatomical make-up. Know your own body and respect its limitations.

1. Start in Easy Pose, with a long spine and grounded sitting bones.

2. On an exhalation, send your right knee far out to the right, squeezing calf against thigh.

3. On an inhalation, flex your right foot and tuck it into the left-hand side of your groin.

4. Keeping your right foot in place, lift your left knee out to the side, flex your foot and place it into the right-hand side of your groin. These movements must come from your hips, not your knees.

5. Place the backs of your hands against your knees, with thumbs and first fingers touching (a gesture called Jnana Mudra).

6. Repeat, starting with your left foot, exiting the posture carefully.

DANCER POSE (NATARAJASANA)
Advanced

Dancer Pose is a standing balance that can be scaled up in difficulty (such as by holding your foot with both hands). Not only does it challenge your balance but it also opens your chest, hips and thighs.

1   From a stable standing position, ground down through your right foot and lift your left heel towards your left buttock. Take hold of your ankle or the top of your foot with your left hand.

2   Pressing your ankle into your hand, use this motion to hinge your chest forwards and lift your left thigh until it is parallel with the mat.

3   Keep extending through your upper body, lifting your chest and stretching your right arm up or in front of you.

4   As you gain confidence in the posture, lift your back foot higher, maintaining that tension against your hand. You can keep a micro-bend in your standing leg for stability.

5   Repeat on the other side.

MONKEY POSE (HANUMANASANA)

Advanced

Monkey Pose is the yogic version of the splits. It is often depicted as a symbol that is the pinnacle of flexibility, since it requires advanced mobility of the hip flexors and hamstrings.

1   Once warmed up, plant your right foot and take a deep step back with the left, then lower your left knee.

2   Keep both hands planted either side of your front foot and your hips even.

3   Straighten through your right leg, sending it out in front of you, and flex your foot.

4   Begin to inch your right heel forwards. It can help to place something slightly slippery beneath your heel, so long as you are in control.

5   You can also inch your left leg back until you are lowered down into front splits.

6   If you are confident here, lift your arms above your head.

7   Repeat on the other side.

EAGLE POSE (GARUDASANA)
Advanced

Eagle Pose improves balance, stretches the upper back and shoulders, and strengthens the lower body, but accessing it requires concentration and coordination.

If you have knee issues, either avoid hooking the ankle or keep your legs in Chair Pose.

1   From standing, squeeze your thighs together and bend your knees (Chair Pose).

2   Pick your right leg up and cross it over your left, as high up as possible. Keep the deep bend and stability through your left leg.

3   Send your right ankle behind your left calf, hooking on to your left shin.

4   Hold out your arms in front of you and cross your left arm over your right. Bend your elbows, bringing your hands towards your face. Try to touch your palms or the backs of your hands together.

5   Keep your chest upright and lift your elbows upwards to feel the stretch.

6   Repeat on the other side.

BIRD OF PARADISE (SVARGA DVIJASANA)

Advanced

Much like Eagle Pose, Bird of Paradise is as much a test on your coordination as it is on your balance, hip and shoulder mobility, and hamstring flexibility.

`There are a few ways to enter the pose, but here we enter from a side lunge variation (Buddha Utthita Parsvakonasana), which is a great preparatory pose.

1   From Warrior 2, in which your right foot is forwards, lower your right arm to inside of your right thigh.

2   Then thread your right arm under your thigh. Send your left arm behind you and take hold of your right wrist.

3   Keeping your arms in this bind, step your left foot up to meet the right.

4   Start to lift your chest, your bound arms bringing your right leg with you as you stand up.

5   Lengthen your spine, send your shoulders back and start to straighten your right leg, pointing your toes.

6   Repeat on the other side.

CROW POSE (KAKASANA)
Advanced

As well as arm strength, arm balances require correct technique, core strength and full-body awareness.

1   Before attempting arm balances, warm up your wrists.

2   Squat down and place both hands on the mat, directly beneath your shoulders with a small bend in your arms, and spread your fingers.

3   With your knees on the outside of your elbows, lift your hips high and send your weight forwards, grounding down into your arms.

4   Begin to squeeze your elbows with your knees, keeping your arms parallel. This motion is key.

5   Keep squeezing and grounding as you tip your weight further forwards until you can lift one foot off the floor then the other.

6   Tumbles are part of the learning process! You may wish to put a cushion in front of you for confidence.

WHEEL POSE (URDHVA DHANURASANA)

Advanced

Wheel Pose (also called Upwards Bow) is a deep backbend, requiring mobility in the shoulders and flexibility of the back muscles. Once it is accessible, it's a great posture to build upper body strength and create space in the ribcage.

1   Lie on your back, knees bent and feet planted. Throughout the pose, keep your feet, knees and thighs in line with your hips.

2   Place your hands either side of your head, palms facing down, fingers pointed towards your shoulders.

3   As you inhale, first lift your hips towards the ceiling. Then press your hands into the mat to lift your chest and head. (You can press up in one movement or pause on the crown of your head, without putting any weight on your head.)

4   Once up, think about lengthening your arms and legs and distributing your weight evenly.

5   Make sure you exit the posture slowly and with control.

HEADSTAND
(SALAMBA SIRSASANA)
Advanced

Headstand should be practised once you're fully warmed up, and in the presence of a teacher until you have become proficient in the correct alignment.

1   From a kneeling position, place your elbows on the mat, beneath your shoulders.

2   Bring your hands forwards to make the top point of a triangle, and interlace your fingers. Tuck your little finger in.

3   Place the top of your head into the triangle so that the back of your head snuggles into your interlaced hands.

4   Straighten your legs and press up onto your toes. Make sure your forearms are grounded and your shoulders strong, protecting your neck.

5   Walk your toes towards you so your hips are over your shoulders.

6   Lift one foot off the mat, tucking your knee into your chest, then the other. When you are ready, extend your legs up above your hips.

ELEVATING YOUR PRACTICE

We have learned some of the foundational yogic principles and physical asanas that are at the heart of many yoga classes, which is a great point from which to begin any yoga journey. Now we will look at the further habits, exercises and points of focus that will allow your practice to flourish.

Throughout this chapter we will explore how breathwork and meditation can strengthen your mindset, and look at the points of focus that extend far beyond asana alignment, including eyeline, hand positions and internal focus. We will also touch upon the importance of creating the right atmosphere – one that is the most conducive to a positive session.

Yoga is an inherently personal activity, and only through dedicated practice will you begin to discover the tips and techniques that best help you to connect with the myriad of benefits yoga has to offer.

WHEN TO PRACTISE

As an ancient meditative art, yoga would be practised for hours on end. In some societies and dedicated ashrams, that is still the case. However, for many people living in the modern world, yoga must fit in around busy work and home lives. Carving out time in the day to breathe, meditate and enter a state of flow can seem a tricky task.

Practising in the morning can help to invigorate you for the day ahead and set your thoughts on a positive path. Practising in the evening is a wonderful way to unwind. It can help clear your head and encourage a more peaceful night's sleep.

The key is consistency and dedication. If you cannot fit a full session in daily, even 5 minutes of meditation before bed or a few minutes stretching while the kettle boils can make all the difference. Remember that you deserve to make time for yourself.

Yoga has been turned into something you can "fit in" to a busy modern lifestyle. But it came from something that was the complete opposite.

JIM MALLINSON

PREPARING YOUR SPACE FOR PRACTICE AT HOME

Yoga requires little more space than that of a mat, making it reasonably easy to practise at home. However, practising in a cluttered or chaotic space can detract from the calming benefits. Here are some ways to prepare your home space.

- If you can, clear space around your mat so that you can flow freely, without the risk of bumping into furniture.
- Turn off your phone and anything else that might distract you.
- If there are others at home, ask for some privacy.
- Ensure the room is tidy and clutter-free.
- Reduce noise where possible. Turn off the TV and close the windows.
- Help create an ambience with mood lighting, candles, incense and gentle music.
- Have any props, a water bottle and clothing layers within reach.

PREPARING YOUR SPACE FOR PRACTICE IN A STUDIO

It can feel intimidating to start at a new studio. Follow these general tips and studio etiquette to help you settle in quickly. Remember that yoga ethics are built on helping others, so don't be afraid to ask for help.

- Outdoor shoes are not usually permitted to be worn in the room where you practise.
- Lay your mat down and prepare any props you may require. Try to maintain some space between you and the mats around you.
- Have a water bottle and clothing layers within easy reach.
- Let your instructor know you're new and tell them about any injuries.
- If you borrow a mat, follow the studio's rules on cleaning it after use. Put all props back where you found them.
- Leave the class quietly so as not to burst the meditative atmosphere.

SOUNDS AND MUSIC

Music can be integral to building or breaking an atmosphere in the yoga classroom.

Different styles of yoga lend themselves to different genres of music, or no music at all. A Vinyasa class may use music to help invigorate during faster flows and to soothe during the most restorative sequences. Ashtanga classes are traditionally practised in silence, save for the sounds of yogis inhaling and exhaling.

Gongs and singing bowls create vibrational sounds to deepen meditation and connect with different energy pockets in the body, and will often be used in yoga classes. Chanting is also a common yogic practice, in which the sounds are used to help focus the mind.

If you're practising at home, music can help you zone in and drown out external distractions. Find a genre or soundscape that helps you to elevate your practice. Remember, the aim is not to drift off but to remain focused on the movement and your breath.

HOW TO BREATHE IN YOGA

Breathing comes naturally to us, but efficient and deep breathing requires attention and practice.

Take time to tune into the rhythm and depth of your breath at the start of a yoga session. Correct alignment is key to creating space for full breaths. Whichever asana you are in, focus on maintaining space around your ribcage (back, front and sides) to fully inflate your lungs.

Ensure your exhalations remain steady, maintaining a constant flow until you have expelled all the air.

Traditionally in yoga, both inhalations and exhalations are performed through the nose unless otherwise specified. *Ujaji* breathing (also called Ocean Breath after the gentle tidal noise it creates in the back of the throat) is used in many asana practices, and is achieved by breathing through the nose and gently constricting the throat. It builds heat in the body and can help externalize where you're at on a breath cycle.

MY BREATH ANCHORS ME TO THE PRESENT MOMENT

*Yoga practice helps
me to stay present and
focus on the now,
which is kryptonite to
my inner saboteur.*

RuPAUL

BREATHWORK PRACTICE: YOGIC BREATHING

This exercise helps to deepen the breath before you begin an asana practice and encourages you to visualize the flow of air. It is a powerful tool to enhance how postures work for you.

1   Find a comfortable seated position, with a long spine and relaxed shoulders.

2   Close your eyes and tune into your breath.

3   As you inhale, imagine the air flowing into your stomach. As you continue to inhale, "watch" the breath travel up to your chest, your throat and your "third eye" (the space between your brows).

4   As you exhale steadily, imagine the air flowing back out through your third eye, throat, chest then stomach.

5   Continue to breathe in this way, imagining the path of the breath flowing up from stomach to third eye, and back down again as you exhale.

BREATHWORK PRACTICE: IN FOR FOUR, OUT FOR SIX

This is a deeply relaxing exercise that calms the nervous system and focuses the mind. It can be done before bed or before a yoga class.

1   Sit up straight, with space around your ribcage and abdomen. Settle into the rhythm of your natural breath.

2   Inhale steadily for a count of four, at a pace that fills your lungs.

3   Exhale smoothly for a count of six, at a pace that expels all air.

4   Continue for as long as needed.

The counts can be altered to suit you, so long as you're keeping the exhalations longer than the inhalations. Any time an exhalation is longer than an inhalation, signals are sent to your brain that everything is OK, which helps you to slip away from a state of stress.

MEDITATION AND YOGA

Meditation and yoga are deeply entwined. It is impossible to have a whole yoga experience without practising meditation. The sole purpose of the physical exercise is to shake out the body to bring you closer to a meditative state. Those who skip the Savasana Meditation at the end of a class have perhaps not done a yoga class at all, merely a sequence of movements.

Meditation does not only mean sitting still and trying to clear the mind; it is the mindset in which you are thinking of nothing but the present moment. So when you are holding an asana and contemplating only your breath and the way your body feels in that moment, that is a form of meditation. It is a discipline that requires plenty of practice but rewards you with immense peace and clarity.

MEDITATION PRACTICE: BODY SCAN

If you find it difficult to stay present during Savasana, try a simple body scan to check in with yourself.

1   Get comfortable. Use any modifications and props needed to maintain comfort and stillness.

2   Bring your "mind's eye" to your feet. Notice the feel of your toes, soles, heels and ankles. Release any tension being held there. Allow your feet to feel heavy and relaxed.

3   Move your focus up to your shins and calves, then knees and thighs, pausing at each point to check in and release anything you're holding on to.

4   Keep slowly scanning all the way up your body, from the tips of your toes to the crown of your head.

5   It is natural for your mind to wander. Any time you notice it has, gently guide it back to a body part.

I ACCEPT
WHERE I'M AT
AND HONOUR
WHO I AM

WARMING UP
BEFORE PRACTICE

Warm-ups are crucial to avoiding injury. Yoga teachers will sequence classes in a way that appropriately warms up the body before attempting peak – or more challenging – postures.

- **HEART:** Gently raise your heart rate with a few Sun Salutations.

- **ABDOMEN:** From a tabletop position, lift your knees an inch off the ground and hold, to fire up the core.

- **HIPS:** Sitting with the soles of your feet together, knees wide (Butterfly Pose) warms up your hip flexors.

- **BACK:** Warm up before full backbends with gentle backbend poses, such as Sphinx and Cobra.

- **WRISTS:** Before arm balances, warm up your wrists with rotations and light load-bearing holds.

Remember to only practise advanced postures once you've warmed up all your muscles to support you, taking extra time to focus on any personal areas of tightness/weakness.

HAND GESTURES (MUDRAS)

Mudras (a Sanskrit word meaning "seal" or "gesture") are the hand gestures that accompany yoga, pranayama and meditation asanas. They are believed to elevate your practice by enhancing the flow of energy, ensuring it is "sealed in" in the right way. During meditation, it can also help to focus on a simple physical sensation.

Here is an introduction to three commonly used mudras:

- **JNANA MUDRA** (the mudra of wisdom or knowledge): Touch forefinger to thumb and extend the other three fingers. Palms face upwards. This gesture represents receptivity to higher powers.

- **CHIN MUDRA** (the mudra of consciousness): Touch forefinger to thumb and extend the other three fingers. Palms face downwards. This gesture is for introspection and grounding.

- **ANJALI MUDRA** (the mudra of salutation): Keep palms together, with thumbs at the heart centre and fingers pointing upwards. This gesture is for connection to yourself and others.

FOCUSING YOUR DRISHTI

Drishti means "gaze" or "vision" and refers to the focal point of gazing in yoga and meditation. Contrastingly, it does not mean "where to look" while in a yoga pose. Since yoga involves the withdrawal of senses, you should not be actively "looking" at all. Consider it more like "a place to hang your eyes", as you might hang up your coat while you practise. Try to soften your gaze, letting your eyes blur over slightly, to help with the sense withdrawal.

Each asana has a suggested *drishti*, and this will often be cued by the instructor, to help with your alignment. For example, in Downward-Facing Dog, the *drishti* is your navel, to help keep your neck long and focus on your belly – your energy centre.

It is also particularly helpful during balancing postures, since focusing the gaze on a fixed point can help stabilize the body.

*Yoga does not transform
the way we see things,
it transforms the person
who sees them.*

B. K. S. IYENGAR

ENGAGING YOUR BANDHAS

The Sanskrit word *bandha* means "lock". The purpose of engaging your *bandhas* is to lock in the precious life force, or prana, that exists within us. Unlike mudras, they are as much a mental focus as a physical engagement. Here are four main *bandhas*:

- **MULA BANDHA** (Root Lock): Engaged by gently drawing up the pelvic floor muscles. To stop the "leak" of prana through the lower body.

- **UDDIYANA BANDHA** (Abdominal Lock): Engaged by drawing the abdomen in and up. Improves diaphragm muscle efficiency and taps into improved self-confidence.

- **JALANDHARA BANDHA** (Throat Lock): Engaged by gently contracting the throat. Relaxes the mind and stops prana escaping through the crown of the head.

- **MAHA BANDHA** (Triple Lock/Great Lock): A combination achieved by engaging all *bandhas* at once.

THERE IS AN ABUNDANCE OF BEAUTIFUL ENERGY WITHIN YOU

PARTNER YOGA

Your yoga journey is personal to you, but that doesn't mean to say it can't be enjoyed alongside others! Involving yourself with your local yoga community is a great way to enhance your connection to the practice, as is inviting loved ones to join you in your practice.

Look out for specific partner classes in-person or online, as these will incorporate assisted asanas, in which you physically connect with each other while practising. This can range from tuning into each other's breath patterns, to holding hands to support and stabilize in balances, to using the weight of each other to deepen folds.

Working with a partner can be an intimate experience of trust and communication, and trying new techniques and pushing boundaries can be good fun. The shared experience may also lead to greater openness and gratitude within your friendship or relationship outside of the yoga classroom.

YOGA AS
A LIFESTYLE

As a yoga lover, it is likely that along your yogic journey you have encountered, and been inspired by, some other yogis who have helped you to fall further in love with the practice. Perhaps they exuded the peace, joy and generosity that arises from a dedication to yoga as a way of life, not just an exercise.

Throughout this chapter, we will explore how you can take your love for yoga beyond the mat and into daily actions and thoughts to live a life of tranquillity, contentment and gratitude.

This will range from simple mindset shifts to habitual actions that can be incorporated into everyday life, and will also include a further look at yogic philosophy and practices, such as chakras and Ayurveda.

While it may take some time to adjust to new ways of thinking, know that you have everything you already need within you to lead a yogic life.

A YOGIC MINDSET:
MINDFULNESS

Mindfulness is paying attention to the truth of the present moment without judgement or interruption from distracting thoughts.

In a physical yoga practice, mindfulness is being entirely present on your mat by bringing your attention to only your breath and asana alignment. It may also involve noticing how you feel internally or emotionally in the moment, without passing judgement on whether those feelings are negative or positive.

Mindfulness is a meditative habit that you can practise throughout your day by focusing solely on the moment at hand. For instance, you can eat mindfully, noticing the flavours and textures, and walk mindfully, noticing the sounds and colours around you.

When you begin to adopt a mindful outlook, you live life more wholly, fully experiencing the world around you and within you at the present moment, rather than your attitude being clouded by perceived judgements and imagined realities.

A YOGIC MINDSET: LOVING KINDNESS

Loving kindness is a way of channelling your thoughts through a lens of love and kindness to all. Employing the loving kindness mindset means being compassionate towards and sympathizing with everyone, even those who hold different belief systems and morals. It is a way of sending benevolence into the world in order to heal hurt and encourage peace.

Loving kindness should also be directed towards the self to overcome negative thoughts and judgements. It can be practised within yoga by always treating your body and mind with love and respect. This means not pushing your body too far or chastising yourself if your mind wanders during meditation.

You can practise adopting this mindset through a dedicated Loving Kindness Meditation, in which you meditate on thoughts of yourself and others, allowing only loving feelings to exist. Let negative thoughts and judgements melt away and be replaced by warm kind-heartedness.

YOU CANNOT
CONTROL
EVERYTHING
OUTSIDE OF
YOU, BUT YOU
CAN CONTROL
EVERYTHING
WITHIN

A YOGIC MINDSET: GRATITUDE

When you start to acknowledge and express gratitude towards everything that life provides you, you will likely find more and more to be grateful for.

When practising yoga, you can find gratitude for a number of things: the physical body that is strong, mobile and able to flow; the time, space and security that permits you to practise; those around you for practising with you.

Try to carry this sense of gratitude beyond the class and into your daily life, feeling grateful for the loved ones in your life, your creativity and wisdom, and the physical items that bring you comfort and joy.

You can even use gratitude to find a ray of sunshine during times of hardship. Try to counter negative spirals by expressing gratitude towards the good, no matter how small it seems, even if that means simply being grateful for the lessons being learned during difficult times.

A YOGIC MINDSET: DROPPING THE EGO

As we have learned, a fundamental ethos behind all that yoga is built upon is acknowledging that we are all part of one whole. In order to fully understand that, we must drop away from a sense of individualism and remove the ego.

In a more literal sense, removing egotism from your yoga practice is hugely beneficial for both mind and body. When you let go of the need to impress others or maintain your pride, it means you start to embody a practice that is more authentically nurturing and truly nourishes the soul.

Abandoning the ego also reduces the risk of injury in yoga, since you listen to your body's boundaries and do not push yourself to accomplish something purely for self-satisfaction. You can achieve this in class by focusing only on your own mat and not comparing yourself with those around you.

KARMA YOGA

You may be familiar with the term "karma" and the idea that our actions have consequences. Karma (derived from the Sanskrit word for "action") in yoga is the path of action that involves selfless service. It involves acting from the heart and without the anticipation of what we will receive in return. Without that expectation, there is a greater sense of peace and acceptance.

To truly practise Karma yoga involves introspection and honestly acknowledging the good deeds you carry out without any interest in personal gain. Think about how you can contribute positively to the community around you in a sincere and selfless way.

Many yoga establishments and training centres run Karma yoga schemes, in which you volunteer your time and energy to help run them, often in return for free classes or training. However, remember that your help should arise from the goodness of your heart, not the expectation of gaining something.

SELF-CARE

To lead a yogic lifestyle means finding the balance between being selfless and free of ego and treating yourself with care and compassion. The limbs of Patanjali's *Yoga Sutras* contain discussions of duties to ourselves, such as *saucha*, the act of cleanliness.

Yoga is a great act of self-care. By practising yoga you dedicate time to improving your mental and physical well-being, but it is vital to ensure that you are practising in a self-compassionate way. Self-care within a yoga setting might mean respecting your body's limitations in asanas or choosing a restorative Yin class over an Ashtanga class if your body calls for it.

By listening to your own needs and taking the necessary acts of self-care in daily life, you will in turn feel healthier, more energized and more able to fully embrace your yoga practice.

One of the most exciting things about yoga is that as I get older I seem to get better at certain parts of the practice.

STING

FUELLING YOUR BODY

For many people, it is not viable to adopt a strict yogic diet due to health reasons, busy schedules and financial factors. However, there are some simple habits you can adopt to eat in a way that will nourish you sufficiently and help achieve a yogic glow from within.

- **MINDFUL EATING:** Take time over each meal to savour the flavours and appreciate the privilege of eating good food.

- **NON-VIOLENT EATING:** Try to incorporate vegan/vegetarian foods as much as possible.

- **AVOID RAJASIC EATING:** Rajasic foods, such as coffee, sweets and some spicy foods, are overstimulating and can cause hyperactivity and trouble sleeping. Eating hurriedly is also rajasic.

- **AVOID TAMASIC EATING:** Tamasic foods, such as deep-fried and processed foods, are hard to digest and can cause bloating and lethargy. Overeating is also tamasic.

YOUR POTENTIAL IS LIMITLESS, AND ONLY YOU HAVE THE KEY TO UNLOCK IT

SLEEPING

Yoga and sleep exist in a synergistic cycle, where one enhances the other.

Sufficient hours of good-quality sleep will leave you more energized and ready to approach physical yoga practice. And in turn, practising yoga can aid deeper, more restful sleep by tiring out the body and calming the mind.

Yoga Nidra (also called Yogic Sleep) is a form of guided meditation, usually practised lying down, that aims to allow the mind and body to enter into a deep state balanced between consciousness and unconsciousness. It can be incredibly healing for those with troublesome sleep patterns.

Pranayama (breathwork practices – see page 91) can also help ease you into sleep by slowing down the mind and calming the nervous system.

Explore which techniques help you to achieve restful sleep and notice how that enables you to commit more energy to building a yogic lifestyle.

CHAKRAS

The word "chakra" refers to the wheels of energy located throughout the body. Understanding the chakra system can be very enlightening, since "blocked" chakras can lead to physical or emotional symptoms.

The seven main chakra points are:

- **ROOT** (Muladhara): At the base of the spine, it helps you to feel grounded, stable and secure.
- **SACRAL** (Svadhisthana): Below the navel, it is responsible for your sexual and creative energy.
- **SOLAR PLEXUS** (Manipura): In the abdomen, it is responsible for confidence and self-esteem.
- **HEART** (Anahata): At the centre of your chest, it is concerned with love and compassion.
- **THROAT** (Vishuddha): In your neck, it's responsible for your ability to communicate clearly.
- **THIRD EYE** (Ajna): Between the brows, it helps you with intuition and imagination.
- **CROWN** (Sahasrara): At the top of the head, it is responsible for your spirituality and sense of connection.

AYURVEDA

Ayurveda is often considered the "sister science" to yoga. It is a natural system of medicine that encourages the maintenance of health and the prevention of ailments through finding balance according to each individual's unique constitutional make-up.

The overarching Ayurvedic principle is that when mind, body and spirit are in harmony with the universe, you will have good health. Therefore, Ayurvedic treatment and prevention are holistic and involve addressing a person's diet, habits and way of thinking.

Ayurvedic practitioners believe every person is made up of space, air, fire, water and earth, which combine in the human body to form the "doshas": Vata (space and air), Pitta (fire and water) and Kapha (water and earth).

Learning which dosha is most dominant in you (which can be done through questionnaires) can help to address areas in which you might be imbalanced and therefore susceptible to ill-health or unwanted moods.

*Yoga is not about
touching your toes,
it's about what you learn
on the way down.*

JIGAR GOR

BE TRUE
TO WHO
YOU ARE,
AND WATCH
THE MAGIC
UNFOLD

INTERACTION WITH NATURE

It is imperative to yogis that they treat the world around them with care and respect, especially the natural world.

Practising yoga outside in nature can deepen your connection to the natural world and elevate your understanding of, and appreciation for, the practice itself.

- Perform standing asanas, including balances, barefoot on the earth to deepen the feeling of being rooted and grounded.

- In lying down postures, look up at the sky to feel connected with the whole universe. This is also a good way to unblock your Throat Chakra for better communication.

- Meditate in nature. Tune into the peaceful sounds around you and appreciate the present moment.

- Practice pranayama techniques in nature to fill your whole body with good-quality air.

RETREATS

Yoga retreats offer an opportunity to immerse yourself in your practice away from the distractions of daily life. They can be transformative experiences and are often spiritually and emotionally enlightening, as well as educational. They can also be a great way to meet others who share your love for yoga.

Retreats can range in duration from one weekend to a week or more and cater to all abilities. Some retreats specialize in particular styles of yoga, while others offer a mix. They can be luxuriously pampering, very modest and traditional ashram stays, or nature-centric and eco-friendly.

Other types of retreats include:

- Silent retreats
- Couples retreats
- Teacher training retreats
- Adventure retreats (with additional sports)

Choose a retreat that will enhance your practice and best serve your needs at that moment in your life.

BERRY SMOOTHIE BOWL

Serves 1

This colourful dish nourishes your body with banana and berry goodness – the perfect way to start your day.

Ingredients

- 1 large banana, frozen
- 80 g (2⅔ oz) frozen raspberries
- 80 g (2⅔ oz) frozen blackberries
- 3 tbsp non-dairy plain yoghurt
- Splash of almond milk (optional)
- 20 g (⅔ oz) cashews
- ½ banana, sliced
- 1 tbsp chia seeds

Method

Add the banana, raspberries, blackberries and yoghurt to a blender and blitz until smooth. If you would like a thinner consistency, add a splash of almond milk and mix again.

Pour the smoothie into a bowl and top with cashews, banana slices and chia seeds.

GRANOLA TO GO
Makes 12

Packed full of nutty crunch and the satisfying sweetness of honey and banana, these balls are perfect to pack for your yoga practice.

Ingredients

- 150 g (5 oz) Medjool dates
- 75 g (2½ oz) granola
- 20 g (⅔ oz) walnut pieces
- 20 g (⅔ oz) dried banana chips
- 2 tbsp raw cacao powder
- 2 tbsp almond butter
- 2 tbsp honey

Method

Place all the ingredients into a food processor and blitz until fully combined (you may need to scrape gooey bits off the base of the bowl every so often).

If needed, pop in the fridge for 15 minutes to firm up.

Squeeze each portion of mixture in your hands before rolling into a ball.

These will keep refrigerated in a sealed container for five days.

AVOCADO AND BANANA SMOOTHIE

Serves 1

This superfood smoothie will energize your mind and body, helping you to get the most out of your practice.

Ingredients

- 1 small, ripe banana
- Flesh of 1 avocado
- 1 tsp lemon juice
- 1 tsp agave syrup
- 200 ml (⅓ pint) almond milk
- 3 ice cubes

Method

Slice the banana then add to a blender along with the avocado and all the other ingredients and blitz until smooth.

Transfer to a glass and serve immediately.

NUTTY BANANA MUESLI

Serves 1

This simple recipe is a nutritional powerhouse bursting with protein and fibre to fuel you for your day.

Ingredients

- 15 g (½ oz) plus 1 tbsp chopped almonds
- 40 g (1⅓ oz) oats
- 3–4 walnuts, finely chopped
- 15 g (½ oz) dried cranberries
- 1 tbsp sunflower seeds
- 3 tbsp puffed rice
- 100 g (3⅓ oz) non-dairy plain yoghurt
- ½ medium, ripe banana, sliced

Method

Heat oven to 180°C/357°F/gas mark 4. Spread out the almonds (reserving 1 tbsp) and oats on a baking tray and toast them in the oven for 8–10 minutes.

Put the oats and almonds in a bowl and mix with the walnuts, cranberries, sunflower seeds and 2 tbsp of the puffed rice. Stir briefly to combine.

To assemble, layer the yoghurt and oat mixture in a bowl or glass. Top with banana slices and the remaining chopped almonds and puffed rice.

CONCLUSION

In reaching the end of this book, you have found the start of your onwards journey. You are equipped with all the knowledge you need to build a holistic yoga practice and watch the magic unfold within you.

You should feel confident in your ability to step further into the world of yoga, be it your first step or your thousandth one. Remember that the yoga community is one of support and care, and everyone is there with positive intentions. Take time to discover a yoga routine that works for you. You will soon learn whether you find practice more beneficial at home or in a studio, solo or with others, in the morning or in the evening, or a blend of them all depending on your needs at that moment in time. That is the beauty of yoga as a practice – it is so fluid and versatile that it can be adapted to serve you in the best way each time. Even if you can't dedicate endless hours towards a physical practice, try to incorporate a little slice each day, such as one Sun Salutation, to maintain your evolvement.

By now you have learned that yoga is far more than just asanas but that they are an integral part. Approach your asana practice with an open heart and a sense of play. Enjoy learning new ways of moving, trying new things and improving in strength and flexibility. With regular practice, you can also become more deeply connected to your physical body. Session-to-session it will feel different. On days when you do not feel as mobile or your balance is off, simply observe that fact and appreciate how you are paying attention to your body, not working against it.

It may feel like there are many things to focus on. Remembering your breathing, your alignment, to be present but relaxed, to be switched on but tuned out... it can feel like a lot! It may help to set an intention at the start of a session; for example, one day focus on engaging your *bandhas*, the next on your posture alignment. Slowly build up the layers of your practice until it comes together naturally.

Most importantly, yoga should make you feel good. Be sure to practise in a way that is safe, healthy and enjoyable for your body and mind. Let it build the light in you so you can shine forth into the world.

Namaste

CREDITS

THE LITTLE BOOK FOR WILD SWIMMERS

Laura Silverman

Hardback

ISBN:
978-1-83799-207-2

Escape the frantic pace of the everyday, reconnect with your wild side and discover the healing power of swimming outdoors

Nature is a balm for both the body and soul – and nothing comes close to the exhilaration of that first stroke in a lake, river or sea. Whether you've already taken the plunge or simply want to dip a toe in, this beautiful book is brimming with all the tips and inspiration you need to harness the invigorating benefits of wild swimming.

Have you enjoyed this book?

If so, find us on Facebook at
Summersdale Publishers, on Twitter/X at
@Summersdale and on Instagram and TikTok
at **@summersdalebooks** and get in touch.

We'd love to hear from you!

www.summersdale.com